More Words of Life

SELECTED SERMONS

Donald G. Hanway, D.Min.

RELATIVE CONNECTIONS PUBLISHING

LINCOLN, NEBRASKA

More Words of Life -- Selected Sermons

Relative Connections Publishing
P O Box 5612
Lincoln, Nebraska 68505-0612
www.RelativeConnectionsOnline.com

Cover Design ©2017 Relative Connections Publishing
Book Design and Layout ©2017 Relative Connections Publishing

Ordering Information:
Quantity sales. Special discounts are available on quantity purchases by corpora-tions, associations, and others. For details, contact the "Special Sales Department" at the address above.

More Words of Life/ Donald G. Hanway. -- 1st ed.
ISBN 978-0-9974250-2-4 Paper
ISBN 978-0-9974250-3-1 Digital

Printed in the United States of America

First Printing July 2017

Contents

Books by Donald G. Hanway

Religion / Spirituality

- A Theology of Gay and Lesbian Inclusion
  - Love Letters to the Church—(2006) ©
  Haworth Press, Inc.

- Words of Life - Selected Sermons — (2009) ©
  iUniverse

Fiction

- Her Appearing — (2008) © Donald G. Hanway
  (Publisher: iUniverse)

- Looking for Home — (2016) © Donald G.
  Hanway (Publisher: Relative Connections)

Foreward

Over the course of my preaching history, I have prepared and delivered somewhere between 1500 and 2000 sermons, not counting homilies for weekdays and sacramental occasions such as marriages and funerals. The first ten years' worth of my Sunday sermons were mostly forgettable. In the second half of my tenure in my primary pulpit, I found my voice and began producing sermons that were more original and impactful. Some of these were included in volume 1, *WORDS OF LIFE*.

Since retirement over 13 years ago, I have done some of my best preaching, albeit in a supply capacity, which changes the dynamic between preacher and listener from pastoral to guest. A number of these sermons are included in this volume, along with a few from earlier.

I was not as concerned in this collection with the flow of the Church Year, or whether certain texts or themes are repeated; in fact, they are, partly due to the circumstance that much of my supply preaching has been done in the summer.

My greatest growth as a preacher, which I hope is reflected in this second collection, comes out of my own spiritual growth, and out of my conviction that in a splintered and increasingly skeptical yet hungry world, an authentic word of Biblical hope is more needed than ever.

A plethora of voices today, on-line and from clashing traditions, threatens to minimize and discredit the preaching office, and many of the rising generation see themselves as too "enlightened" to make any attempt to integrate Sunday School faith with their other learnings. Nevertheless, the witness of countless contemporary saints continues to inspire those of us who have given our lives to the holy calling of preaching the Good News in our time.

Author's Preface

This second collection of my sermons, a sequel to *WORDS OF LIFE* (iUniverse, 2009), spans the thirty-five-year period from when I returned to my home-town to take on the combined parish and campus ministry that was to occupy two-thirds of my full-time ministry.

Nearly half of these sermons were prepared and delivered in a supply capacity, post-retirement. Nearly all are based on the three-year Lectionary contained in *The Book of Common Prayer 1979*. Nearly all were preached in Lincoln, though not all in the same pulpit.

The occasions range over the entire church year, and present a variety of topics. The length varies. Many were preached in the summer, when parish clergy are seeking a substitute so they can go on vacation. There are some references to current movies, but not as many as in the first volume. Some themes and some scripture texts are repeated, hopefully with new insights each time.

Preaching, in retirement, has continued to be my most satisfying ministry, and an offering I continue to take seriously. The Word of God is more than words in a book—it is a Living Word that addresses each of us personally: encouraging us, challenging us, and calling us to share our gifts with the world. I have been blessed to be a long-time partner in this ministry.

Donald G. Hanway

Shrove Tuesday, 2017

Sermon One

Accepting the Challenge

August 2, 1981 (Year A) My First Sermon at Saint Mark's on the Campus

A young man fresh out of seminary was preaching for the first time in the church where he had been hired as a curate, and he asked the wise, old rector for any advice he might have. The older man said,

> *"Preach about God, and preach about ten minutes."*

This *is* a sermon about God, and it may run just *over* ten minutes.

The propers today have a *lot to say* about God: about how He remains faithful even when His people are unfaithful; about how Jesus is our assurance that nothing—not even death—can separate us from God's loving care; about how God both purifies and protects His people, in spite of their lack of faith. But I want to *focus* today on the *Gospel*, which shows God's concern for both the physical and spiritual needs of His people, and His ability to work miracles with a small amount of faith on our part.

The account of the feeding of the multitude—which appears in *all four* Gospels—portrays a movement in the experience of the disciples. A movement from *doubt*, to *obedience*, to *wonder*—a movement that I also see in my *own* life. It is a movement from faith *challenge*d, to faith *exercised*, to faith *expanded*.

Faith is *much more* than a *warm feeling*. It's more like a *muscle*—that grows and keeps fit only as it is *used*. The faith of the disciples was challenged when they went to Jesus, pointing out the lateness of the hour and the almost total lack of food service facilities. There wasn't even *one* pizzeria nearby, let alone *four*! But Jesus said to his disciples,

> *"You give them something to eat."* (GULP!)

Immediately there was doubt. Could the challenge be met? Their faith was being tested.

My faith was challenged when I got a phone call asking if I would interview here at St. Mark's. Frankly, not only was I not ready to move, I hadn't *thought* of myself as a college chaplain.

"You give them something to eat."

I asked myself if my few loaves and fishes would be enough. This was certainly an opportunity to *grow*; it was also an opportunity to *fail*. What would people here expect of me? Would they be disappointed? I knew the men who had been here ahead of me.

The *disciples, too*, must have questioned the wisdom of arousing people's hopes of being fed, only to disappoint them. The twelve probably would have said "No" if the *people* had asked, but it was their *Lord* asking them. They didn't have a *lot* of faith. They had just enough to be obedient—to offer their few loaves and fishes—to do their small part—to exercise their faith. Somehow, they must have known that if all those people were going to be fed, God was going to have to do it. This *is* God's Church. And when God asks us to do something, we'd better try to do it.

When I think of the name of our newsletter, "The Lion's Roar," I think not only of St. Mark the Evangelist, and of George Peek, the latter-day lion incarnate, but also of a verse in the Book of the Prophet Amos: (3:8) "The lion has roared; who will not fear? The Lord God has spoken; who can but prophesy." "*You* give them something to eat."

We would have nothing to give, if God had not already given it to us first. But until we offer it *back* to Him, not much will happen. After I got the phone call, I thought about it. And I realized that unless I gave it a shot, *I would never know* what God might be able to do, through my (few) loaves and fishes—and I would be the loser. For God can always find a way to feed His people. We, on the other hand, lose our way unless we follow where God is leading. If we exercise faith, it grows in us. If we do not,

Faith withers and dies. The disciples, in spite of their doubt were obedient—and God multiplied their offering a thousand-fold so that there was more than enough. Their *faith*, then, was *likewise* multiplied and transformed from doubt to *wonder*.

This feeding of the multitude had all the marks of a *Eucharist*. It was *introduced* by the Ministry of the Word, as Jesus taught. Then he *took* the gifts that were offered, *gave thanks* to the Father, *broke* the bread, and *distributed* it, with the disciples acting as deacons. *And*, the Gospel says, "they all ate *and were satisfied*." Was this purely a *spiritual* satisfaction, or a *physical* satisfaction as well? The *answer* is provided by the *left-overs*—a basketful for each of the twelve disciples, or the twelve tribes of Israel. It was a feeding for the *whole* person, body and spirit, and for the whole people of God.

As I come to St. Mark's on the Campus, I am filled with wonder at what God is *already doing* and *has* done here through the men and women who have offered themselves. My faith is strengthened as I see God feeding His people. And I see His concern to feed people both *physically* and *spiritually*. I am glad that St. Mark's has a Pantry Program, and that the congregation cooperates actively with other churches and groups seeking to meet a variety of human needs. Yet I am keenly aware that our main reason for being here is to share that *living* bread which came down from heaven and gives meaning to all our other sharing. People come to Jesus for something to which they can commit themselves, as well as for their daily bread. That's why the whole multitude came out in the *first place*.

What was the role of the disciples, and what is our role here at St. Mark's? First—to recognize the many human needs that exist, and to share these with our Lord; and secondly—to share the many gifts of God with people. In other words, our role as a congregation is a priestly one—offering *ourselves* in the lifting up of *man to God*, and *God to man*. We should expect great things from God in this enterprise. We *can* have confidence that He will provide more than enough, as long as we continue to offer ourselves in obedience.

When were the loaves multiplied? Not *before* the distribution, but in the *act* of distribution. Spiritual gifts increase as we use them. If we want a blessing from God, we must give Him something with which to work. St. Mark's faces great challenges, financially and spiritually. As the faith of the people of Israel was forged at the crossroads of travel and commerce, amid the struggle for supremacy of the great world powers, so we exist here at the crossroads of a dynamic city and university, and with the eyes of the Diocese upon us. We'll be O.K. *as long as we remember* our *true* source of nourishment.

There is a song which I got very *tired* of singing in the early 70's, at youth camps and conferences. The *song* may not be fresh, but the meaning of the words is as fresh as ever: "He's Got the Whole World in His Hands." Of course, if He's got the whole world, he's got the itty-bitty babies, and you and me. He's got St. Mark's on the Campus in His hands. He has St. Mark's firmly in his grasp because He cares for all people, and for *all their needs*. God will look out for His Church not because he loves those outside it any less, but because the Church is the chosen and created instrument of His greater purpose for human life. God wants us to *see* what He is doing in the world and to be a *part* of that. He says to us: "*You* give them something to eat." As we hear and respond, we will find our faith challenged, exercised, and expanded. We will move, not just once, but again and again from *doubt* to *obedience* to *wonder*. And we will *know* that He is God.

Sermon Two

What Do You Mean, "Jesus is Coming"?

December 1, 1985 (Year C) Advent I

A professor in a small college in North Carolina, who teaches a course in New Testament literature, was asked by a visiting parent what approach he took in such an introductory course.

"Do you start with Mark's gospel?"

"Oh no," said the professor, who was also a Presbyterian minister. "We dive right into the Book of Revelation. I know that's a mind-blowing experience for everyone in our 20th Century rational American culture. But I'm convinced it reflects the 1st Century Jewish mindset better than any of the others. I want my students to make that startling discovery first, so they won't think the gospels and letters can be read as though they were straight out of our own time. The apocalyptic mentality is present in and through all the New Testament writings. We need to look at these from a perspective foreign to our own, in order to understand them on their own terms."

The lessons today have such an apocalyptic flavor—"apocalyptic" meaning the revealing of things which have been hidden, referring to matters of the coming of the Messiah and the end of history. Jesus' talk in the Gospel about reading the signs that the end is near, just as people know that summer is near when the fig trees leaf out, has inspired many contemporary Christians to look at current events for clues that Jesus is coming.

The recent earthquake in Mexico, the volcanic eruption in Colombia, the threat of worldwide financial collapse, and the escalating arms race give some Christians a curious kind of comfort. as they see these events all as signs that Jesus is coming soon. Of course, not everyone is so pleased—especially teenagers.

In a recent interview in Time magazine, Garrison Keillor, creator and star of the "Prairie Home Companion" radio show, was asked about his experience growing up in a small fundamentalist church. He said, "I remember, when I was fourteen years old, hearing people talk about the 'Lord's coming' and the fact that it could occur at any moment and all I could think of was I hoped God didn't come until I had . . . (sampled certain earthly pleasures) . . . because I wasn't sure they would be a part of heaven. In fact, I strongly suspected that they *wouldn't* be."

I think it was St. Augustine who prayed, in the same vein: "Lord make me holy—but not too soon!" Whether we hope Jesus will come soon, or would prefer that he wait a while, there is a natural human tendency to protect ourselves from surprises—either by trying to read the signs, or by pooh-poohing the whole idea.

The possibility that Jesus may come at a time we do not expect is not entirely welcome news to *any* of us. In fact, as Charles Reich pointed out some years back in his book, *The Greening of America*, a book that was naïve in some ways but right on target in this respect: people will go out of their way to avoid being surprised. Reich wrote:

> "If there is one characteristic that is shared by all different groups . . . aircraft employees, old leftists, young doctors, Kennedy men, suburban housewives—it is the insistence on being competent and knowledgeable, on having 'already been there.' The aircraft worker, if he is a weekend camper, knows all about boots, camping equipment, maps, trails, and weather. The young lawyer's sophisticated wife converses about Camus, The New York Review of Books, and Mozart at a dinner party, and she speaks with the same knowledge and assurance that the aircraft worker has in his own area of interest. Her husband is an excellent tennis player or skier. The professor of law knows all about the latest theory of pluralism and the latest development in mergers; he seems to listen at a cocktail party but really does

*not; there is nothing for him to learn. Mention sex,
restaurants, travel, everybody knows all about them.
One can't tell them anything; they adamantly resist
and belittle any new information or experience."*

(I interrupt at this point to ask: "Is this only the Eastern elite
that Reich is describing? No, I think you can find the same thing
in the Midwest and I have seen it—uncomfortably—in myself.)

Reich goes on:

*"At social gatherings the conversation reveals all
of this clearly. Sometimes it is a display of what the
speaker knows. At other times, two people agree on
what they know—'we understand' the subtleties of
skiing or tennis, [or football?] they say to each other.
There may be an argument about who knows the
most. But rarely is there someone who is unprotected
and undefended, unprepared for anything that may
happen."*

The Gospel says that the signs 'of Jesus' coming will be unmis-
takable. But might it be different from what we expect? Are we
open to being surprised? Throughout his ministry, Jesus lamented
the blindness of those who could not see what was happening
before their eyes. How might our expectations be getting in the
way of our readiness to welcome Jesus? For one thing, what is the
main feeling you get when you think of the Second Coming? Is
it *excitement*, or *dread*?

Out of the recent semi-voluminous literature on the Near-
Death Experience, an article popped up in the Lincoln Star last
Friday, pointing out how widespread the experience of transcen-
dence *is*, and the impact that it has on people. Those who have had
such an "out of the body" experience are no longer afraid of death.
Without going into the whole subject at this time, the thing that
strikes me at the moment is this: that which was *feared* turns out to

be a *blessing*. What would it be like if we stopped thinking of the Second Coming, primarily in terms of cataclysm and judgment, and thought of it more in the terms of *joy* and *fulfillment*?

C. S. Lewis somewhere in his writings says that when we meet God, it will be an encounter with Light [rather like the "Being of Light" described in many of the Near-Death Experiences?]. God will welcome us in all of his glory, His love and compassion and unconditional acceptance. We, however, according to how we have lived life here, may throw our arms over our face to protect ourselves from the light, and then retreat from God to the place where we feel comfortable. But if we have been walking in the light, we will find it natural, and walk into the arms of perfect Love.

So the Second Coming may be *different* from what we've imagined. It may be a gracious reality—depending on what we're *looking* for. And finally, it may come in the midst of our own *personal* upheavals. The message of the Gospel is that *when the worst happens*, remember that a loving God is still in charge. The Jewish symbols of cataclysm—the sun and moon being darkened, stars falling from the heavens—are indeed foreign to our thinking. But every one of us, if we live long enough, has or will come to times in our own little worlds, if not in the larger one, when the foundations of life are shaken and the worst happens, or threatens to. The doctor says, "It is cancer, and there is nothing more we can do." Parents are told, "Your new baby has this rare condition, and the odds are not good." Someone close to you dies in an accident or has a heart attack. You lose your job, or have to move, or your best friend moves away. Or the heavens shake as you hear the words "I want a divorce." When the worst happens and the ground seems to give way beneath our feet, and the world no longer seems safe or manageable, where do we turn? What is there to hang onto? Who or what can be trusted?

The message of Advent is not a promise that our world will *not* be shaken. It *is* a promise that when the worst happens, a loving God is still in charge. The Lord who comes is a Lord of love, who can transform and redeem even the worst of situations, bringing new life out of death, new hope out of the ruins. The same God, who scientists now tell us, has created the most mathematically improbable physical coincidences both in the macrocosm and in the microcosm, in order that life as we know it might come into being, has come to be with us and will be there when our world crumbles.

As we light the candles progressively each week, let us look for the coming of the One who is the Light of the world, in the faces and events of our own. Then we will never need to say, "What do you *mean*, 'Jesus is coming'?" We will recognize the One whom we have known, who has already come to us.

Sermon Three
"The Boundless Sky"
May 22, 1988 (Year B) Pentecost

"When the day of Pentecost had come, the disciples were all together in one place. And suddenly a sound came from heaven like the rush of a mighty wind . . ." And there was *communication*—a breaking down of the barriers of language and culture.

Norman Pittenger tells of a child who asked a wise old pastor: "*Where does the sky begin?*" And the pastor replied: "The sky begins in your lungs." How do we begin to connect with the vastness of God? Pentecost tells us that God becomes known when we begin speaking to one another in a way that gets through. Communication is a *gift*, and a *mystery*. We are invited to be partners with God in that work of breaking down the barriers.

This week saw a couple of tragic examples of *non*-communication, close to home. On Tuesday night, someone broke in to the lounge at St. Mark's and ruined several inside doors in a search for money and frustration at not finding much. We could have told them they were wasting their time and saved us all a lot of aggravation, not to mention the cost of damages. Perhaps we need to put a sign out explaining what churches have and don't have on the premises. I don't know. Sometimes it seems that the more we help, the more people want. One-way communication always has an element of violence. One party is saying: "Here is what I want to do. Here is what I *need* from you." But there is no message being heard the other way: "Here is what *I* need. Here is what I can do for you." We live in a broken world, where there are vast communication gaps; and as I said last week, some of these are in the Church.

The other recent, vivid example of non-communication was at the Lincoln Fellowship of Churches spring delegate assembly this past Thursday night. Two messages were being sent. But neither side was hearing the other very well. One message was: "If we are a fellowship of *churches*, what does that *mean*? What is it that binds us together, that gives us our *identity* as churches? Is it not a common loyalty to Jesus Christ? We are certainly open to working with other groups in a common concern for human needs, but we need to be clear about what brings us together." The other message was—(I'm over-simplifying, of course): "Our mission is to serve the world by ministering to human need. How can we get hung up on creedal statements that serve only to exclude some groups that might otherwise want to be a part of our mission and fellowship? Should not our focus be on the *work*, rather than on who we are?"

Right now it appears unlikely that a compromise can be found which will keep everyone within the fold. We will either define "church" in a way that excludes non-Trinitarians, or we will adopt *no* statement and lose one or more congregations who are charged by their parent groups with limiting their ecumenical participation to Christian bodies. If we could keep the dialogue going, I believe that the Spirit could show us the way. But people become impatient and communication stops, and fellowship is broken.

"Where does the sky begin?" We have to keep the conversation going. But the *breakthrough* into real understanding—we cannot make that happen. Only *God* can enable us to find a unity in diversity, so that we can appreciate and use all our gifts. Pentecost reminds us that God's boundless energy of love is available to us, and can make a difference.

What do we have to do to tap into this energy? That very question suggests a possible misunderstanding. It is not God who is at *our* disposal. It is *we* who are to put ourselves at *God's* disposal. And when we do, great things can happen. "When the day of Pentecost had come, the disciples were all together in one place . . ." They had made themselves available to God and to one another. They were keeping the lines of communication open. And the boundless sky of God descended and gave life to their utterance. The Spirit and their breath became one.

"The sky begins in your lungs." It is the sky that we need, to lift us above our differences. But that sky begins in our lungs. The Spirit of God enlivens the Word of God and our words and makes communication possible. The great wind of God can transform the brokenness of violence into the connectedness of peace. And Jesus said to his disciples: "Peace be with you. As the Father has sent me, even so I send you."

Your lungs are needed to give voice to the sky—even as your ears are needed to hear the wind of God blowing through other lungs. As we make ourselves available for the divine work of reconciliation, we will find a *new* language. It may be a kind of music, as the young David calmed the torment of King Saul by playing the harp. Or it may be the language of touch, which transcends so many barriers. Whatever your new language is, don't be afraid to speak it and offer it in God's service. For from God all things come and to God all things return, and we are all one in the boundless sky.

Sermon Four

"Burning Bushes"

May 29, 1988 (Year B) Trinity Sunday

"The bush was *burning*, yet it was not consumed." On this Trinity Sunday, I invite you to think with me about how God is revealed to us. We live in a world that is *full* of burning bushes; but most of them are *invisible* to us. We pass them by without a nod. So the very *first* challenge in the process of revelation is to get our *attention*. We are so used to taking miracles for granted—both in the natural order and in the technological order. It takes something *really* out of the ordinary to get us to turn aside. Or maybe we have to be standing at just the right place to see something we have passed by many times before and realize that something *marvelous* is happening.

I was at Lincoln General Hospital the other day, on one of the upper floors, waiting for the elevator—which if you've been there much you know can often take a while. And I was looking out through the window on the north side of the hospital. I've looked out many times before. There are many things to look at out that window. But this time I happened to look down at the grass—and I saw the *wind* blowing the grass, in shimmering waves. It was a most amazing sight. Seeing it was a matter of being at just the right distance, I think. Fortunately, the elevator didn't come right away, so I had a chance to concentrate on the grass. And I wondered why I hadn't seen that wave motion before.

You've seen the ads on television. They begin with a person that we don't recognize, asking: "Do you know me?" Then we get a clue based upon what the person has done or regularly does. We may or may not guess who it is, from that. Finally, we watch as the person's name is typed in raised lettering onto an American Express Card. And *then* we *know* who it is. It's a twist on our usual experience, which is seeing a face that's familiar and struggling for the name. Here the face is new; at first there is no reason to know the name. And that's a lot like revelation. We don't even *connect* what we're seeing—at least initially—with God. All we know is that it's something that we've never really seen before—even though we may have passed by it many times. And then we get a clue as to who is *behind* what we're seeing. And finally, the name clinches it.

"Do you know me?" Yes, Lord, we know you. But we do *not* know all your faces. God the Father remains hidden. It will take a burning bush for the invisible to become visible for us. Moses was just looking after his father-in-law's sheep. He had no intimation of an appointment with God. But here was this amazing sight, that he had never seen before. So Moses said: "I will turn aside and *see* this great sight, why the bush is not burnt. The first challenge of revelation is getting our attention. But once we have *given* our attention, the second challenge follows immediately. Because the *object* of our attention may be a *problem* or a *puzzle* for us, which may not be so easily resolved. We can hardly believe what we're seeing. And so a *decision* is called for. Do we trust the reality of what we're seeing? Or do we *dismiss* it, because it makes us *anxious*, and go back to *not* seeing? Everyone knows that if bushes burn, they burn *up*. Do you want to *mess* with one that *doesn't*?

A little old lady in Boise, Idaho put a classified ad in the paper to sell a low-mileage, nearly new Cadillac for only $50. A lot of people noticed the ad. But it was a while before anyone called. Why? Well, come on! If someone's selling a nearly-new luxury car for next to nothing, there's got to be a *catch* to it. The offer is inviting, but also *threatening*. If I get too *close* to this burning bush, *I* may get burned! Finally, someone checked out the Cadillac ad and found out it was *genuine*. It turned out that the lady had a good *reason* for selling the car so cheaply. She had been recently widowed, and her late husband had specified in his will that the car—*or* the proceeds from the sale—were to go to his *girlfriend*.

The burning bush was a *problem* for Moses. It shook up his convictions about reality. He had to make a *decision*: either to *expand* his view of reality, or to retreat into some *dismissal* of what he was seeing. When God is revealed to us, we have the same choice. And the burning bush above *all* burning bushes is *Jesus*. You can't really be neutral about Jesus. Either he is risen from the dead and speaks the words of eternal life, or you have to *diminish* Him and *distance* yourself in some way. We are invited to take off our shoes and enter into dialogue with the mystery of the bush which burned and yet was not consumed—this life which was laid down and was taken up again. And if we *do* stand our ground, revelation can go a step further. The bush can become for us the gateway to new life.

God spoke to Moses out of the bush and said: "I am the God of your father, the God of Abraham, the God of Isaac, and the God of Jacob." The raised letters appeared on the American Express card, and Moses knew who he was dealing with, and he hid his face. God is a consuming fire. But it is not enough to *recognize* God. Somehow, we have to let the fire of God into our lives. And that is *threatening*. It is also, when it happens, a *revelation* which completes the Holy Trinity. The work of the Holy Spirit is to enable us to interact with the invisible that has become visible in such a way that we are energized but not destroyed—set on fire, but not consumed.

John Wesley was once asked about the secret of his preaching. And he said, "I set myself on fire, and people come to watch me burn." We don't have to set *ourselves* on fire. That is the work of the Holy Spirit. We *do* have to turn aside, first of all, to see God's presence among us—the extraordinary in the ordinary. We live in a very sacramental world. As Elizabeth Barrett Browning wrote: "Earth's crammed with heaven, and each common bush is aflame with God. Yet only he who sees takes off his shoes. The rest set round and pluck blackberries."

We have to stop, turn aside from all our preoccupations, and see that the place where we are *standing* is holy ground. And then take off our shoes, and enter into dialogue with the Holy

One. We have to decide whether or not we will allow our view of reality to be revealed as insufficient—or whether we will *deny* that possibility. The God that is hidden in this world—and hidden in *us*—may become known—if we will allow it. The fire that burns without consuming stands before us and offers us the possibility of being transformed—of becoming who we are really meant to be.

As Moses' life was radically changed when he turned aside to see the burning bush, so that his subsequent meetings with God would light up his face, and also that his life would be poured out in God's service—so your life and mine are like kindling waiting for the torch. Can we trust God to set us on fire and yet preserve our lives?

Sermon Five

"Living in the Open"

June 12, 1988 (Year B) Proper 6

Pick up a newspaper. Turn on the news on television. Living in the world is an insecure proposition. Everyone needs to find a place of shelter, not just outwardly, but inwardly. We need some protection from the elements. But there is a wrong way and a right way, to go about making a home in this world. We need to know our true situation. And, very simply, it is this: this world offers no secure place of refuge. We are, all of us, street people—living in the open.

It was the summer before my senior year of seminary. I had come back to Nebraska to visit a friend, out in Central Nebraska, and he was driving me around. We were in the vicinity of Cozad when a thunderstorm came up. I remember how *exposed* I felt. There was such a contrast between Virginia, where I had been living, with all the trees around and being out on the plains of Nebraska when a storm came up. I was reminded very dramatically: *out here there is no place to hide.*

St. Paul expressed a similar idea when he wrote: "Here indeed we groan and long to put on our heavenly dwelling, so that by putting it on we may not be found naked. For while we are still in this tent, we sigh with anxiety. . ." Hearing his words, I remember also the experience of the people of Israel, whose forty years in the wilderness, on the way to the Promised Land, became a central part of their spiritual understanding. Those were hard times. But they learned something about their true situation in this world. They learned that there was no place to go for help except God. In their insecurity and vulnerability, they learned to depend upon God. It was a lesson they were later to forget. Here in this world we are out in the open—exposed to the storms of life. The only shelter we have is tents—*temporary* dwellings. And a strong wind will blow them away. That is the truth about our life. We have to depend upon God.

There are some stronger souls who have tried to live *apart* from God. They are like the towering cedars of Lebanon, sending their roots deep into the soil of this world, and pushing their tops high above the daily struggles of other mortals. They have been respected as benefactors. They have been lauded for their achievements. The storms of life do not sway them very much. They regard themselves as self-made, and look down upon the less successful. They deny their dependence upon God. But they, too, are vulnerable. Listen to what the prophet Ezekiel has to say about the proud and independent people or nations of this world, "Therefore thus says the Lord God: Because it towered high and set its top among the clouds and its heart was proud of its height, I will give it into the hand of a mighty one of the nations. . . Foreigners will cut it down and leave it. . . Its boughs will lie broken in all the water-courses of this land; and all the peoples of the earth will go from its shadow and leave it."

Toppling the mighty has become a national pastime, in our day. There is no particular virtue in cutting down a cedar of Lebanon. We could name many such trees—many such persons—that have fallen in recent years on the national scene. We are sobered when we realize that this great country of ours could face a similar fate. If we deny that God is the true source of our blessings, and if we continue to insist on maintaining our national prestige and standard of living, without regard for the needs of the developing nations, *we will fall*—aided by more vigorous new economies, such as those in the Far East. Living in the open—*apart* from God—is a dangerous illusion. The cedars of Lebanon will fall.

But there is another way of living in this world. There is a way to make a home which acknowledges our true situation and builds not upon pride, but upon faith. That is the way of the mustard seed. By itself, the mustard seed is *nothing*—a tiny speck, easily blown away by the wind. But when it is planted, an amazing thing happens. Out of insignificance emerges a ministry of integrity. Out of the small acts of kindness which we regard as nothing, a living organism takes shape. The tiny mustard seed becomes, not a towering tree, but a generous and hospitable shrub—in fact, the greatest of *all* shrubs. It becomes a place of community, offering shade, and a place to perch. It is still out in the open; but no one is going to cut it down. The Kingdom of God, said Jesus, is like a mustard seed.

We can despise the abilities and opportunities which God has given us to serve and to grow. After all, they seem so tiny, and so problematical. Or we can be faithful and obedient. We can plant our little seeds, and give them time. Some of them may be completely forgotten. But one day we are astonished to find that God has been doing something. Almost behind our backs, it seems, the seed has been growing. And the result is marvelous. People are brought together. Gifts are multiplied. Human needs are met in surprising ways. And all of this is out in the open, without any greenhouse. But you have to plant the seed. And that is an act of faith.

We live in insecure times. Sometimes it seems that our whole world is coming apart. Certain it is that human empires will crumble. But in the midst of it all—right out in the open—God is doing something remarkable. People like you and me who have no illusions that, individually or corporately, we're going to be cedars of Lebanon—people like you and me, who know our vulnerability and put our faith in God—people like you and me are planting tiny seeds. And God can use our little acts of faith to grow a place of shelter and human community—a preview, if you will, of the community which is to come and of a home which will be secure. For now, we must be content to live in the open. But keep on planting those seeds.

Sermon Six

"Lever or Lover?"

July 31, 1988 (Year B) Proper 13

The big event was over. The crowd had been fed. Many of the people had gone home. But some of them got into boats and came across the lake to see this wonder-worker again. They wanted to get a handle on the power he had displayed. And Jesus sized up their motives pretty quickly. What they were looking for was not really what he was offering. So he *challenged* them—he challenges *us*—saying: "You seek me, not because you saw signs, but because you ate your fill of the loaves."

Right now is an "in-between" time for many of us. For some of us it's right before vacation or right after vacation. School is coming again soon. For the Episcopal Church, it's not only right before another year of programming, but right after the General Convention, whose decisions and actions remain to be interpreted and implemented. There is a hush of suspense, waiting to see when the first woman bishop in our communion will be consecrated, and how everyone will react. It is a time for all of us—students, workers, church people—to step back for a moment and take a fresh look at what we are up to. What is it that we hope to achieve? After what are we striving? And the Gospel today asks us a very pointed question: in our view of the world, the church, and our place in all of it, who will be in control? Whose hand will be on the lever? Is it God's Kingdom that we are seeking, or a Kingdom of our *own*?

In some ways the culture of Jesus' day was very different from our own. But in at least one important way, it was very much *like* ours. Then, as now, people had a hunger, not just for bread, but for some *control* over their lives. "Freedom" is the word today. We want to have *options*. We want to own the *language*. We cherish our right, every four years, to "throw the rascals out"—or to keep *out* the *pretenders* to the throne. Our *real* control over what is going on is more an *illusion* than a reality. And in that we are not so different from those people who come after Jesus. They were looking for a leader who would make a *deal* with them. They would do certain things; the leader would do certain things. In short, they would know where the lever was and how to pull it. Jesus would be a King of *their* creation. They had no *inkling* of who Jesus *really* was, or what he *could* be to them.

Notice the *dialogue* that takes place between the people and Jesus. Jesus says: "Do not labor for the food which perishes, but for the food which endures to eternal life, which the Son of man will *give* to you . . ." What is their reply? They say: "What must *we* do, to be doing the works of God?" The focus of Jesus is on what *God* is doing. The focus of the people is on what *they* will do, in order to have a lever—some *claim* upon God. They did *not* see what the feeding of the multitude *meant*. Jesus sees their misunderstanding, but replies to their question in this way: "*This* is the work of God, that you *believe in him* whom he has *sent*." But they are still looking for a lever—a lever that will be in *their* hands. So they say: "Then what *sign* do you do, that we may see, and believe you? What work do you perform?"

They are thinking of Jesus as a possible successor to Moses, who provided manna in the wilderness. Jesus says: "Truly, truly, I say to you, it was not Moses who gave you the bread from heaven; my Father gives you the *true* bread from heaven." And *they* say: "Lord, give us this bread always." *Put the lever into our hands.* And Jesus says: "*I* am the bread of life. . ." And they don't know what he is talking about.

Jesus doesn't need their vote in order to be King. He is already a King. Jesus doesn't need their works as part of a *deal* to give them security. What Jesus is offering is much *more* than what they are *asking*. They are looking for a lever. Jesus is offering them, instead, a *lover*.

Yes, the Red Sea and the Manna—the sacraments of the Israelites—were great. But what Jesus is offering—the new sacraments of baptism and the Holy Eucharist—the water and the bread of new life in union with *Him*—are so much greater. There is a tremendous gap here. It is a gap between two ways of looking at the world and at God. And I would submit that the same gap—the same conflict—exists today. People have not changed that much. Now, as then, people have aspirations to be in charge of their own lives. And this is not totally illegitimate. It's very understandable. It's understandable because of all the helplessness and uncertainty we endure as human beings in a world of powers that are not so friendly to human welfare. We *want* to get our hands on the levers, to stop some of the abuses, and to abate our fear and our anger. And *God wants* us to claim our rightful stewardship in the face of dehumanizing forces. But there is a right way and a wrong way to set right the evils in this world. And no matter how attractive it looks, the wrong way will never work. That is the way of the lever. It will not work, because it provides no basis for unity or communion.

We all want to get our hands on the levers. We all understand the problems differently. So no matter how well orchestrated the convention, whether it is the Democrats in Atlanta or the Episcopalians in Detroit, the differences remain. And it is only the way of Jesus that can bring us together. Can we make the leap between our way and His way?

I think we can take a cue from the new science of chaos which was highlighted in an article in the Lincoln Star this past Tuesday. Scientists have been focusing, for a long time, on finding the regularities in nature and trying to overlook, or downplay, the *ir*regularities—those annoying exceptions and unpredictabilities that act like monkey wrenches in all our grand systems, and some of our less grand ones, such as weather forecasting. Now there is a revolution underway. Scientists are beginning to take those random instances—those puzzling complexities of nature—and to see them, not as aberrations, but somehow as part of a larger design whose outline we do not yet comprehend.

Scientists would no doubt describe the implications of all this differently than I do. But just as we have seen, and are seeing, a revolution in physics and mathematics in our way of looking at the world, so—I would submit—we stand on the threshold of a revolution in our relationship with God—as did those people who followed Jesus across the lake. It is the leap between looking for a simple magic formula that we can manipulate, and accepting what God has provided. Picture again those people talking to Jesus. Jesus says: "This is the work of God, that you believe in Him whom He has sent." The people respond: "Then what sign do you do, that we may see, and believe you?"

Remember this is *after* Jesus had already fed the multitude. But they missed the point. A commentator has this observation to make about those people—and I would say about us: "To them 'belief' meant acceptance of his competence on the basis of the miracles; to him it meant commitment, not finally on the basis of the miracles, but on trust in his person. . . He desired that (men) should receive Him, not simply for what he might *give* them, but for what He might *be* to them." It's a long way from: "what sign do you do, that we may see and believe . . .?" to: "I am the bread of life. . .." It's a long way from a religion where we are in control and earn our way, to a faith in a God who remains sovereign and gives us much more than we could have expected, asking only our trust in return.

It's a long way from a *leve*r to a *lover.* But that's the choice. That's the invitation. That's the bread which can give life to the world.

Sermon Seven

"A Larger World"

September 18, 1988 (Year B) Proper 20

What's wrong with people? In all the scriptures for today we read of base human motives.

- *"Let us lie in wait for the righteous man, because he is inconvenient to us. . ."*
- *"The arrogant have risen up against me, and the ruthless have sought my life. . ."*
- *"they were silent; for on the way they had discussed with one another who was the greatest."*

Jealousy, vindictiveness, pride—are these the fruits of human life?

A UNL professor recently surveyed his students and discovered, once again, a shockingly high number reporting that they had been victims or perpetrators of sexual assault, among other offenses. Clare Booth Luce wrote several years ago: "Campus surveys show that one third of our college students say they would cheat if they were sure they would not be caught.

> *"Forty-five percent say they do not think it is necessary to lead a moral life in order to be happy or successful."*

Dr. Will Herberg, the late social philosopher, said:

> *"Today's culture comes very close to becoming a non-moral normless culture."*

Clifford Goldstein, in an article in *LIBERTY* magazine suggests that the new political activism of the religious right wing in America is not the sign of a spiritual revival, but an admission of weakness. He says:

"That Robertson, LaHaye, and other Christian
leaders see the state as the necessary vehicle for
Christians to bring moral change is an admission of
spiritual failure."

Robert Coles, a child psychologist who teaches at Harvard says that many parents are confused about what to teach their children. We want our children to be concerned for others; but we also want them to be successful. And sometimes these values are in conflict. When kids are moved to act on the values they hear in the Gospel parents are often embarrassed and say "Hey: don't take us that seriously!"

What's wrong with people? We are an acquisitive, addictive, anti-authority society, capable of good deeds but also of looking the other way; professing high ideals but also secretly believing that people will not do the right thing unless compelled to do so. And if scripture is a reliable authority, we are not so very much different from people long ago. Perhaps we live in a more permissive society. But there has always been a lawless element in our make-up. That's what Original sin means. Obviously, we will not get far simply lamenting our deficiencies. So let us consider not only our need for a stronger value system, but also the roots of ethics and what really moves people to change.

Let's begin by asking the real question behind our addictive society, which I believe is this: *WHY ARE WE HERE?* It's a religious question, perhaps the fundamental religious question. The roots of ethics are religious. Otherwise ethics has no roots at all. *WHY ARE WE HERE?* What is it that we're really reaching out for, as we try to grasp the world and stuff it into our mouths, or up our noses, or into our veins, or into our houses, or into our résumés, or into our wallets, or wherever?

Some years ago there was a song: "What's it all about, Alfie?"—from a movie starring Michael Caine. Alfie was a Peter Pan adult, who enjoyed playing with women but ran from commitment. And as a consequence, a human life was taken. Too late he learned his own tragedy. Alfie was in many ways a parable of rootless ethics. He had no idea "What it's all about."

Let's move closer to home. I'd like to talk about education, but first about a *barrier* to education. And that is our established *dogmas* that are very well-entrenched among many of the custodians of higher education. I encountered these dogmas myself as a graduate student in philosophy across the street twenty-two years ago—dogmas like "If you can't verify it by an experiment, it's meaningless." The evidence is that the dogmas are still with us. As reported by George Cornell, Ben Johnson, a Lutheran clergyman with a doctorate from Harvard, has been doing research in middle America, and his results are echoed by other researchers. What has he found? Many Americans—as much as a third of those surveyed—report paranormal experiences suggestive of a spiritual world about which science knows very little. As a result, Johnson says, "the nation is living with a split between scientific belief and personal reality." While the established view is, academia rules out the possibility of the supernatural, people are having supernatural experiences. It's a real scandal!

What are the implications of this conflict for education? A couple of years ago, I guess, some professors here at UNL were going through a process of asking what it is we're trying to do in education. What are the qualities of an educated person? I sat in on some of the discussion and made a few notes. Here is what one of the professors, for whom I have a great deal of respect, suggested. An educated person:

- *Should be without fear of the new and different*
- *Should be able to think in different disciplines, and to transfer learnings from one discipline to another*
- *Should know himself or herself as a Nebraskan, an American, and a world citizen*
- *Should know how to play with ideas*
- *And should be able to use symbol systems (i.e.,*

languages, mathematics, etc.).

If these are the goals of a liberal education as opposed to a purely technical education, then it seems to me that the custodians of education need to model the same values. We need to challenge the dogmas to which we ourselves have unquestioningly subscribed. My own list of desirable qualities for an educated person, apart from the ability to write coherently and to break a complex problem down into manageable components, would include the following:

- An ability to appreciate other viewpoints, and to understand the process by which views are formed
- A critical awareness of one's own assumptions, and the way that assumptions dictate conclusions
- And a realization of the interrelationship between ethics and ontology or religion, that is, between one's view of what ought to be and one's belief about ultimate reality.

Education can be one tool for helping people break out of the constricting "boxes" of worldviews which are too small into a larger world which makes room for God. But education alone isn't enough. As William Carlos Williams once put it, "Smart doesn't necessarily mean good, not by a long shot." Robert Coles says that his students have reminded him that they can write a brilliant paper on "moral reasoning" and still be, as one put it, "the same old out-for-myself-in-the-clutch person."

What's wrong with people? We need to know why we're here. And that knowledge comes by grace, not just by study. Fundamental change in people happens only when we are loved. Johan Boger's novel, The Great Hunger, published in 1918, was the story of an engineer whose little daughter was killed by a neighbor's dog. That cruel loss turned the community against the dog's owner and tested the father to the limits. Shortly thereafter the region was stricken with famine. The engineer took some of his meager supply of seed corn and planted it in the field of his neighbor whose dog had killed his little girl. Why did he do it? Here is what he said:

> "Now it was that I began to realize how every great sorrow leads us to the outermost port. . . I understood how blind fate can strip and plunder us of all, and yet something will remain in us at the last that nothing in heaven and earth can vanquish. Our bodies are doomed to die and our spirits to be extinguished, yet still we bear within us the spark, the germ of an eternity of harmony and light for both the world and for God.

"Therefore, I went out and sowed the corn in my enemy's field *THAT GOD MIGHT EXIST.*"

Why are we here? We are here to be the receivers and the bearers of grace, that God might exist, not only for us and our loved ones, but for our neighbors, near and far. What's it all about? Grace is what it's all about—love that we don't deserve, but which we get anyway, and of which we are privileged to be stewards. What's wrong with people? Only that their world is too small. It hasn't yet been opened up by challenges to their world-view and by love. God, open our eyes and our hearts to a larger world. AMEN.

Sermon Eight

"The Why in Wine"

January 9 (Year C) Epiphany II

Little kids like to keep the conversation going. And a big discovery for them is the question "Why?" After a while adults cheat and answer "Because." But at first it's great. You can't *really* give a *short* answer to a "why" question unless you say, "I don't know." So it's a set-up for the adult ego. So much return on such a little question!

When we look at the Gospel for today–the first miracle of Jesus, at the wedding in Cana–the wrong question to ask is "How?" The *proper* question is "Why?" Little kids have got it right. "Why?" is the fundamental religious question. Why suffering? Why beauty? Why am I here?

Let's go to the wedding feast, because we can ask the question *there at least six times*. First of all, why *have* a party? A wedding is *serious*, isn't it? Perhaps the underlying question is really: "Why *play*?" Christianity has been made by some into a *deadly* serious business. I was reading the other day about a father who introduced his five-year-old girl to the Gospel by first putting the fear of hell into her. (He did a good job, too.) That's *child abuse* in my opinion. Wes Seeliger had it right when he said that building conversion on the fear of hell is like operating a protection racket. No, I don't think that's what God had in mind in creating us. The German poet, Schiller, stated profound truth when he said

> *Man is only a man when he plays. In play we break into freedom toward the fulfillment of life; and, in the fullness of this freedom, joy comes into the heart.*

God *wants* us to have joy. Because only then do we get a glimpse of why we were created in the *first* place. But, my goodness, if I keep giving such long answers to these short questions we'll *never* get through this sermon!

The next question is" "Why was the *wine* at the celebration important?" Think of a small town, where pretty much everyone knows everybody else. A wedding is a big deal for the family in that community. Hospitality was very important in the Near East at the time of Jesus. To run out of wine for one's guests was to fail in an important obligation and to bring shame on the family for years to come.

Next question: Why did Jesus first react as he did when his mother told him, "They have no wine."? His comment can be variously translated, but is something like this:

> *"What is that to me and to You?" or perhaps:*
>
> *"Why is that our problem?"*

He adds cryptically: "My hour is not yet come." Scholars have speculated as to why he seemed to put her off. His reply seems flippant and disrespectful. But perhaps, in the light of his additional comment, Jesus was saying something like this:

> *I'm not a magic button that you can push*
> *whenever you need something. That's not why I'm*
> *here. My purpose is yet to be revealed. Don't force*
> *me into a grandstand show that is premature and*
> *misleading.*

Remember that Jesus did not always do just what people expected him to do. But when he saw a need that was legitimate for him to meet, he responded. And so he does this time. Of course, Mary knew that he would. She knew something of the character of her son by this time. So to the servants she said, quietly and confident: "Do whatever he tells you."

Next question: Why start with *water*? Let me suggest *three* reasons. First, it gave *others* a part in the action. Someone has asked, "What would have happened if the servants had *not* filled the jars?" Would Jesus have found another way? Or would there have been no miracle? There is a possible teaching here about prayer and our role in what God wants to do. As someone once put it: "Without God, we *cannot*, without us, God *will* not." Notice secondly, that there were *six* stone jars. The Jewish number for perfection is seven. Six falls short, just as water is prized less than wine. The message may be: our imperfection, through God's action, is turned to perfection. But third, we are taught here not to despise the ordinary. It can be a vehicle of greatness.

I have recently read, in serial form, Andrew Greeley's new book, *"A Catholic Theology of Popular Culture."* His point throughout is that popular culture, including everything from Bruce Springsteen to The Far Side to Ellis Peters *can* be revelatory of what God is doing in the world. Not that *every* movie or comic strip is worthy of attention. But popular culture is not to be despised as *inherently* inferior. There is trash in the *classical* genre of music or literature, just as there is trash in rock and roll. *Why start with water?* Because water is what God gives us to work with. The ordinary is not to be despised.

Just two more questions. Why *this story?* It's becoming more clear. This first miracle of Jesus is said by the evangelist to be a "sign," which manifested the *glory* which was in Jesus. It was an "epiphany: or a showing forth of who Jesus was and what he was about. The point of the story is transformation. God can change our water into wine–and Jesus is the key. Marriage, for example, becomes something greater than the sum of two persons when God's synergy enters in. The focus of the story is not on the miracle of water into wine but on Jesus.

This story is an introduction to Jesus. And once we know him, we don't ask "How?" Any more. The story took place, the evangelist tells us, "on the third day"–presumably of the marriage feast. But the third day is also the day Jesus rose from the dead. And ever since then there have been miracles all over the place.

As one recovering alcoholic memorably put it, "I don't know about changing water into wine, but in my family He changed beer into furniture."

So—last question—why invite Jesus to parties? That's easy. First, he's comfortable there. Second, he's good to have around when things don't go as you planned. And third—and most important—Jesus doesn't just *add* something to the party; he transforms *everything*.

Sermon Nine

"More Than a Job"

May 14, 1989 (Year C) Pentecost

Nora Watson says, in Studs Terkel's book, *Working*: "Most of us are looking for a *calling*, not just a *job*. Most of us have jobs that are too small for our spirit. Jobs are not *big* enough for people."

Are you looking for a calling, a vocation, that is more than a job? In Christ you *have* one. Jesus says: "He who believes in me will also do the works that I do; and greater works than these will he do, because I go to the Father." Our vocation, as members of the Body of Christ, is to be doing the works of Christ—wherever we are. Pentecost is the day we especially celebrate, not the *commission* to do those works, but the *power* to do those works. Our calling is to do the works of Jesus by the power of God.

Wind, fire, inspired speech—these phenomena in the Book of Acts were all signs of God's presence and activity. The word for "wind" in Hebrew and Greek also means "Spirit." The wind was coming up; the Spirit was blowing. The inspired speech was a sign that something out of the ordinary was happening—just as Ziggy one time poured milk on an imported cereal, and it spoke in a foreign tongue: "snäp, craeckle, pøp!" The tongues of fire resting on each of the apostles were a sign that the empowerment involved a *personal* relationship with God. Have you ever been on fire for God? Was it more than just emotion? God's power is channeled in all kinds of ways, some of them pretty spectacular, others very quiet.

St. Paul lists some of the gifts of the Spirit:

- The utterance of wisdom
- The utterance of knowledge
- Faith
- Gifts of healing
- The working of miracles

- Prophecy
- The discernment of spirits
- Speaking in tongues
- The interpretation of tongues

With regard to that last gift. . . . Little Marvin is playing with his blocks while his grandfather is reading the newspaper. Little Marvin is making strange and wonderful new sounds: "Ba-boo ga-da! Gibba goba bwam wago! Do-da coo zerp paw-paw na boo!" His grandfather, who evidently has the gift of interpretation says: "Bea, come quick! Marvin just said '*Grandpa*'!"

Now are *all* the gifts of the Spirit on this list from Paul? If you've watched Johnny Carson much at all, you know the answer: "Well, not quite *all* the gifts!" How about the gift of hospitality? That should be on the list. How about the gift of cheerfulness? How about the gift of generosity? I think we could add many other gifts to the list.

Surely the work of mothering is empowered by the gifts of the Spirit. Caring for a demanding child is not a natural talent, I think, for anyone. There is something *supernatural* about how a mother can intuit what is going on, or maintain her poise in the midst of total chaos. And surely the gift of faithfulness is the work of the Spirit. No one is more faithful than a mother, except God herself. Paul's list of gifts is in 1 Cor. 12. The next chapter, we recall, tells us about the greatest gift of the Spirit: the gift that is the key to all of the other gifts—the gift of agape, or self-giving love. The real Pentecost takes place when that gift takes root in our hearts, and directs all the other gifts. To some degree it is not surprising that we love our children, even when they are unlovable. But to love a stranger who makes demands on us—or to love those who do not love us back—this is the sign of a fire that is more than human.

Chuck Irish says that there are three conversions that must take place in us in our Christian development. The first is a conversion to God in Christ that's when we really hear the Gospel. The second is a conversion to the Church, the Body of Christ. That's when we love the brethren, and begin to see what the sacraments are about. And the third is a conversion to ministry—to doing the works of Christ. It is only when we have accepted our calling that we know the love of God in its *fullness*.

In our Christian journey we hear first of all the marvelous news that God loves us: that God sent His Son to die for us, and that Jesus was raised from death as we will be raised. Then we discover that the Church is our family—in spite of the strange relatives we find there. But it is only when we are led into service that is more than we can do in our own strength or love or wisdom, that we can fully know the riches of God. It is when we know at one and the same time both our utter helplessness and God's command and sufficiency that we are born from above.

As Julian of Norwich wrote—I'm paraphrasing—love is what it's all about. Love is the message, and the purpose, and the power. Love is the beginning and the end, and what enables us to live at every moment in between. Love came down at Christmas, but also at Pentecost—the same love. Our calling—the job that is big enough for us—is to be agents of that love. What are some means by which you can do that?

One of the simplest yet most profound ways of expressing love is to spend *time* with people. For a child, or for a person at any age, time *equals* love. That's part of what mothers do: they spend time with their children—more than fathers do, usually. You can't spend a lot of time, obviously, with very *many* people. But you can look around and see who really *needs* your time. Give what you can. And God will be at work in you, multiplying your efforts.

What other gifts can you give? You can give the gift of forgiveness, though you do that as much for your own benefit as for anyone else. You can give the gift of faithfulness: keep your promises; be dependable. You can give the gift of prayer—a gift we often forget or minimize. You can give the gift of encouragement: a letter, an unexpected gift, or helping out in some way. Use your creativity, that's God's gift. All these are expressions of love—signs of God's presence and power. They are the wind of God. They are fire.

Is your job too small for you? Make it bigger. You have a *calling*, issued in your baptism. You probably have a certificate to prove it. Be the Church. Do the works of Christ by the Power of God. And the same breeze that refreshes others through you, the same fire that warms others through you, will also bless you.

Sermon Ten

"Baptized to Serve, Baptized to Die"

January 7, 1990 (Year A) Epiphany I

John said to Jesus at the Jordan: "I need to be baptized by you, and do you come to me?" Jesus answered: "Let it be so now; for it is proper for us in this way to fulfill all righteousness." The baptism John offered was a baptism of repentance—a cleansing of sins. The baptism Jesus accepted was an identification with us, in *our* sins; but it was also something more—an acceptance of God's purpose for His human life.

To be "righteous," in the Biblical sense, means more than just doing what God expects. It means being in right relationship with God—a relationship of trust that issues in obedience. Jesus accepted his vocation, which was to be a servant, and to give up His life in that service. How do we relate to that?

The Holy Eucharist we celebrate each Sunday has been called "the repeatable part of baptism"; it is our food for the journey of living out our baptismal vows. We are baptized only *once*, because we only *need* to be baptized once. We are joined in that gateway sacrament to Jesus, our Lord and Savior. What we do for the rest of our lives is rededicate ourselves to Him, and learn more and more about what our baptism means.

One thing it means is that we have a call to ministry—a call we hear clearly at times, *not* so clearly at others. Our call, if we dare to believe it, is *not* so much different from the call of Jesus. Jesus was called to *die*. And in a real way, we are too.

I'd like to draw a contrast between two scriptures which relate to our baptism. They are like two poles of a larger truth. One is the psalm appointed for today: a portion of Psalm 89. This is a "royal psalm." It speaks of God's anointing of David, the greatest King of Israel, prior to Jesus. By extension, it refers to the anointing of Jesus with the Holy Spirit in His baptism, and to *our* anointing in baptism. The pouring out of the Spirit is empowerment for ministry: it is not given simply to make us feel secure, approved, or superior. No, the Spirit is given to equip us for servanthood, and for faithfulness even unto death.

Psalm 89 is a victorious psalm: David *triumphs* over his enemies. His dominion extends the territory of Israel and Judah within the Near East. The Kingship of Jesus is rather different. He triumphs in a different way, and His dominion is far greater.

The scripture I would set alongside Psalm 89, for purposes of contrast and illumination, is not in the reading today, but we read it every year at the First Mass of Easter, immediately following the Great Vigil. It is from the Epistle to the Romans, Chapter 6, and reads in part: "Do you not know that all of us who have been baptized into Christ Jesus were baptized into his death?" A bit further on it says: "But if we have died with Christ, we believe that we will also live with him."

What is Paul saying? Very simply, the doorway to a greater life is death—here and now, not just at the end of our lives. The life of Christian discipleship is a life of dying and rising. Most of us will do this not once, but *many* times—though it may well be that we will come to see a time in our life as the turning point.

Oswald Chambers, in his classic book of daily readings, *My Utmost for His Highest*, says bluntly in his entry for January 15th, written to spiritual procrastinators: "We skirt the cemetery and all the time refuse to go to death. It is not striving to go to death, it *is* dying—'baptized into His death.' Have you had your 'white funeral,' or are you sacredly playing the fool with your soul? . . . do you agree with [God] that this is your last day on earth?"

The difference, you see, between Christianity and Judaism, is not a difference in devotion to God, or in suffering for God. The difference between Psalm 89 and Romans 6—and I think it is a decisive one—is that Christianity sees death, not as a defeat but as a doorway to victory. Death is not the *end*, but the *beginning*.

John Westerhoff, Episcopal priest and Christian educator, a few years ago, observed a baptism in a small church in Latin America and tells the story, in these memorable terms: "the community of faith had gathered, they had recalled God's gracious acts; they had proclaimed the Gospel. And now they were about to make a response. The congregation began the mournful sounds of a funeral hymn as a solemn procession moved down the aisle. A father carried a child's coffin he had made from wood; a mother carried a bucket of water from the family well; a priest carried their sleeping infant wrapped only in a native blanket. As they reached the chancel, the father placed the coffin on the altar, the mother poured the water in the coffin, and the priest covered the waking baby's skin with the embalming oil. The singing softened to a whisper. The priest slowly lowered the infant into the coffin and immersed the child's head in the water. As he did so, he exclaimed, 'I *kill* you in the Name of the Father and of the Son and of the Holy Spirit.' 'Amen!' shouted the congregation. Then quickly lifting the child into the air for all to see, the priest declared: 'And I *resurrect* you that you might love and serve the Lord.' Immediately, the congregation broke into a joyous Easter hymn."

Good theater, right? It gets to the essence of what our baptism means.

I was recently given a copy of what I think is probably Ken Wilber's greatest book—and that's saying a lot. Ken Wilber, for those who haven't made his acquaintance yet, is *not* what you would call a popular writer. He *is* one of the most wide-ranging and profound thinkers of the twentieth century—one of the few people able to integrate the complexities of the many contemporary branches of human knowledge, including religion as well as the sciences.

The book I read recently is a new edition of *The Atman Project*, and if I may presume to boil down its thesis, it would be something like this: our spiritual odyssey is a journey toward union with God, a journey that must result in the surrender of our ego autonomy—in other words, our death. We resist that requirement, and while we *are* resisting, pursue many God-substitutes.

Now Wilber is a Buddhist. But what he says is what our own Gospel is saying. If we would find the truly abundant life, the price is our death. And as the ad says, *"You can pay me now or pay me later!"* That's *not* the Good News, I venture to say, that most people are ready to hear. We will come to hear it in our own good time—in God's good time. But there is at least the possibility that some here today may be ready to hear it.

Our God is compassionate. Our God is wonderfully patient. Our God continues to call us, to live into our baptism. We can begin doing that in down-to-earth ways that are *not* so diffi-cult—giving attention, showing kindness—learning to surrender to God's will, God's project of the moment, in place of our own. And in due time, God will lead us to the place where we are ready, and by His Grace, able, to yield ourselves fully. Then we shall know the sufficiency of His love.

Sermon Eleven

"Following the Lamb"

January 7, 1990 (Year A) Epiphany II

"There goes the Lamb of God." And his two followers took notice. They decided to *follow* the Lamb. Jesus saw them and asked what they were looking for. They couldn't quite put it into words. What they said, in effect, was: "We want more than a one-time encounter, we want to know where we can *find* you, so that we can come to *know* you." So they asked where he was *staying*. And Jesus said, "Come and see"—an invitation which was to have the most profound impact upon their lives. One of the disciples was Andrew. The other may have been John, the writer of the Fourth Gospel.

The hunger—and the invitation: these are the twin forces which move the true disciple of Jesus. One is inward—the hunger to know God—to find the answer to those burning questions like "Why am I in this world?" and "Why *is* there a world, anyway?" The other force comes from outside the disciple. It is a call—an invitation— "Come and see." Find out yourself what it's all about through personal involvement. But discipleship turns out to be a long journey. When you decide to follow the Lamb of God, you will have to decide, not once but many times, how far you are willing to go.

In his powerful, historical novel, *Silence*, the Japanese Christian Shusaku Endo tells the story of Fr. Sebastian Rodrigues, a Portuguese missionary priest who was smuggled into Japan in the early 17th century, after Christianity had been outlawed. Fr. Rodrigues quickly learned that his own hunger and dedication were dwarfed by the hunger and dedication of those to whom he came to minister. The true martyrs were not those who were caught and made to renounce their faith, but the Japanese people who paid the price of sheltering them. These people endured torture and death—yet remained faithful. The Japanese authorities were very clever. If they killed the priests, they would make martyrs of them. This would only intensify the devotion of the people. So what they did instead, at least with Fr. Rodrigues, as Endo reconstructed it, was to force the priest to face an agonizing choice: either to remain true by not trampling on the sacred image of Jesus, while Japanese Christians, within his hearing, were tortured in punishment for his obstinacy; or to give up the sanctity of faithfulness, in order to spare the suffering of these people. Martyrdom, in other words, could be purchased not with his *own* suffering, but only with the suffering of others. So the choice was between martyrdom and compassion. The question Fr. Rodrigues had to ask himself was: "Which is the true following of Christ?"

What does it *mean* to follow the Lamb of God—the innocent one who suffers for the sake of others? Through his ordeal, Fr. Rodrigues came to a new understanding of sin. "Sin, he reflected, is not what it is usually thought to be; it is not to steal and tell lies. Sin is for one man to walk brutally over the life of another and to be quite oblivious of the wounds he has left behind." There was no way he could ignore the suffering of these people. The real torture for him was to see that their suffering was linked to his own refusal to trample on the face of Christ. And so, in the end, Fr. Rodrigues gave up his good name and the dignity of martyrdom and became labeled as a Judas. Only he—and God—would ever know that he was still a true disciple.

The amazing thing was that when the moment come when he had to symbolically renounce Christ by trampling on the picture of his Lord and Savior, the face of Jesus looked back at him and said, "It is to be trampled by you that I am here." And as Endo describes that moment: "He had lowered his foot on to the plaque, sticky with dirt and blood. His five toes had pressed upon the face of one he loved. Yet he could not understand the tremendous onrush of joy that came over him at that moment." And afterward, Endo writes: "He loved [Jesus] now in a different way from before. Everything that had taken place until now had been necessary to bring him to this love."

Fr. Rodrigues discovered through becoming a casualty—a failure in the eyes of the world—the love of God in Christ for sinners. He learned what it meant that Jesus was the Lamb of God. And he learned what it meant to *follow* the Lamb.

The prophet Isiah writes of the experience of God's call to Israel, the chosen servant—and the servant's lament: "I have labored in vain. . .." This was surely the cry of Fr. Rodrigues many times, as he lived out the twilight of his years in disgrace, as a political prisoner—a subversive who had been crushed, but was not allowed to return home, either, and so had to live as an exile. "I have labored in vain. . .." *Not so*, Fr. Rodrigues. *Not so*. You were an arrow in God's quiver, hidden away for His Glory.

As St. Paul writes to the Corinthians in our epistle today: "God is faithful, by whom you were called into the fellowship of his Son. . .." The sacrifice of a Fr. Rodrigues will not be ignored. We, too, like the missionaries and martyrs of Japan, and the Christians in Corinth, are "called to be saints," called in other words, to be dedicated to *God's* use—*God's* purposes, not our own. And if that means being a failure in the eyes of the world, well, so be it. Success—*even in Christian terms*—is not where the true faithfulness lies. Only God really knows who is faithful. And the hunger—and the call—are the same today.

Albert Schweitzer concluded his book, *The Quest of the Historical Jesus*, with these words:

He comes to us as One unknown, without a name, as of old, by the lakeside, He came to those men who knew Him not. He speaks to us the same word: 'Follow thou me!' and sets us to the tasks which He has to fulfill for our time. He commands. And to those who obey Him, whether they be wise or simple, He will reveal Himself in the toils, the conflicts, and the sufferings which they shall pass through in His fellowship, and, as an ineffable mystery, they shall learn in their own experience who He is.

Sermon Twelve

"Burning Questions"

February 4, 1990 (Year A) Epiphany V

The scribes and Pharisees were striving to know God's Law and to *do* God's Law. But Jesus said, "Unless your righteousness *exceeds* that of the scribes and Pharisees, you will never enter the Kingdom of heaven." Sounds pretty grim. What is the *greater* righteousness? We *have* a standard. But Jesus is *more* than a *standard* of righteousness, or right standing with God. Jesus not only *fulfills* the will of God, being the light of the world; Jesus offers us the chance to be light as well. If we are plugged in to Jesus, we *will glow.*

St. Paul tells us that it is by the Spirit of God that we get the light. No one understands God *except* God. When we begin to get a glimmering of what God is up to, it is because God is moving in us. The prophet Habakkuk says:"

> *"I will rejoice in the Lord, I will joy in the God of my salvation:—even in hard times.*
>
> *"God, the Lord is my strength; he makes my feet like hinds' feet, he makes me tread upon my high places."*

As the current song says, "We didn't start the fire." It was already burning. But if we would find the high places which call *us*—the answer to those burning questions like "Why am I here?"—then that same fire has to burn in us.

The Gospel today tells us that ministry is not an option. If you maintain your connection to Christ, you will burn with the light that is in Christ. If you are a Christian, you cannot avoid being a Christian minister. So you cannot have it both ways. Do you want to stand back, away from the fire? Then you will not be a glowing ember. But if you get close enough to burn, you will serve.

Light has to be what it is. So does salt. In its pure form, salt is a seasoning for food. When it gets mixed with dirt, its usefulness is more limited. It can still serve—to melt ice—when it is "trodden under foot." But its primary usefulness is gone.

The Church is like that. We can serve the world in one of two ways. If we remain unadulterated, we can serve as seasoning—giving the world a flavor it badly needs, such as in ethics. If we lose our singlemindedness, we can still serve—but on the world's terms, not on God's terms. We are trodden under foot and *used*; we do not make a witness.

If you want to burn with intensity and purity—if you want to be pure salt—then it is necessary to *pursue* those burning questions and focus on the *essentials*. What is our purpose? The Westminster Catechism says that our chief purpose is to "glorify God and (to) enjoy (God) forever." In other words, if you turn it around, we are to burn—and in the process, to be a light. How can we do that? The Church has provided everything we need. We have the Sacraments, especially the renewing sacrament of the Holy Eucharist. We have the Word of God, which can nurture us if we will feed upon it. We have the Holy Spirit to illuminate the Word. We have prayer, both private and corporate. We have community, both in the liturgy and in our informal sharing. And we have opportunities to *serve*. The way to be salt and light is to *use* all of these resources.

If you would burn—if you would give *everything*—you must receive a lot. You must receive *continually*. A wick without the wax cannot sustain itself. You have nothing to give, except your willingness to burn. That is your share in the "greater righteousness." But if you *have* that hunger, God will feed you. God will *pour* the fuel to you and through you—to light you and to light the world.

It is a great privilege and joy to be a light. But burning is a *fearful* prospect to contemplate. When we are standing *back* from the fire we see that we will lose *control* over our lives. We see that there will be nothing left. *Everything* will be offered to God; what will be left of us, when we are finished, besides a burned-out wick? Will we then be *abandoned*? These are burning questions.

What happens to that light that is given away and goes forth into the world? That, my friends, is the mystery. If we trust God, we believe that light is not lost. Our burning is not in vain. All love comes from God and returns to God. Nothing is wasted except that which is withheld. We may not see the results of our own ignition. We do see the flames of other candles. And all the lonely candlelight vigils are one great bonfire that shall never be extinguished. We have the privilege of being a part of that fire.

Peter Milne was a missionary to the New Hebrides. When he arrived there the people were cannibals. Those who came after his death found a worshipping community. And the words the people had put under his picture were these: "When he came there was no light. When he died, there was no darkness." So Jesus says to you and me: "You are the light of the world."

Sermon Thirteen
"When Good Things Happen"
March 25, 1990 (Year A) Lent IV

Nobody likes a wise guy. And while the Pharisees were quizzing the formerly-blind man, he got off a couple of real zingers. They said to him, "What did he do to you? How did he open your eyes?" He answered them, "I have told you already, and you would not listen. Why do you want to hear it again? Do you, too, want to become his disciples?" (RIM SHOT)

They reviled him, saying "You are *his* disciple, but *we* are disciples of *Moses*. We *know* that God has spoken to Moses, but as for this man, we do not know where he *comes* from." The man answered, in a voice no doubt dripping with sarcasm" "Why, this is a marvel! You do not know where he comes from, and yet he opened my eyes. . . . If this man were not from God, he could do nothing." It's no *wonder* they threw him out of the synagogue!

But it's not just what he *said* to them. It was the healing *itself* that was the sore point. They had this man *tagged*—and now he wasn't going to stay in his *place*. When *bad* things happen to *good* people, we get *upset*. But when *good* things happen to people we have written off, it can be *just* as upsetting. Something is *wrong*, they thought. It must be a *trick*. God wouldn't do this—*would He?* The assumption they were working on was that if the man had been truly born blind, it must have been God's will. Was God now having a change of heart? The disciples of Jesus evidently shared the same assumption, as revealed when they asked: "Who sinned, this man or his parents, that he was born blind?" Jesus answered, "It was *not* that this man sinned, *or* his parents. . . ." Nevertheless, he goes on to say, God can be glorified in this affliction.

In 1852 Franklin Pierce was elected President of the United States. He was on his way to Washington for the inauguration, on a train with his wife and son, when the train was derailed and wrecked at Concord, New Hampshire. Their son was killed. The wreck was due to the carelessness of an intoxicated brakeman, and several damage suits were brought against the railroad. Mrs. Pierce, a strong Christian, refused to let her husband be a party to a lawsuit. Why? Because she believed that this tragic accident could somehow be used to God's glory. It would serve to keep the president aware of the suffering of others.

Does that mean that God *planned* the accident? *No.* Nor did God plan for the man to be born blind. But these afflictions had the possibility of serving as occasions for God's love and power to be known.

Jesus said, "We must work the works of him who sent me, while it is day. . .." And what *are* the works of God? The 23rd psalm gives a pretty good summary. God is a shepherd, whose work includes:

- Making provision for the necessities of life (vv. 1, 2, and 5).
- Providing guidance, including correction where necessary. (v. 3) The shepherd's staff which bishops traditionally carry has a crook on one end, and a point on the other, so that they can restrain the impetuous and prod the recalcitrant.

God's work as a shepherd also includes:

- Protection from enemies (v. 4)
- Reassurance (v. 4)
- Revival (v. 3)
- And healing (v. 5)

All these ministries are right there in one short psalm. The problem is, that we're not always sure, at any given moment, what God is *up* to. Some things that look like blunders or utter tragedies turn out to be for our good, after all.

A woman was driving home one evening when she noticed a big truck behind her, following very close. She speeded up, but so did the truck. She exited the freeway. So did the truck. She made a turn; the truck followed. By this time she was in a panic.

She whipped into a service station and jumped out of the car, screaming. The truck driver jumped from the truck and ran to the car. Yanking open the back door of the car, he pulled out a man hidden in the back seat. From his high seat the trucker had seen the would-be rapist concealed in the woman's car.

The sons of Jesse were paraded before Samuel, and none of them were chosen—until David appeared. Samuel was as surprised as anyone. But God's word to him was: "the Lord sees not as man sees; man looks on the outward appearance, but the Lord looks on the heart." We see only the appearance of things. We don't know how God views the situation.

Let's go back to the story of the healing of the man born blind. At one time or another, we play all the parts in this story. We are the ones who are questioning what God is doing. We are the parents who don't want to get involved. We are the blind man before and after the healing. And we are also the one who *brings* the healing. If you doubt that, stick around.

Frank Laubach once said: "When Christ, who is the way, enters into us, we become *part* of the way. God's highway runs right through *us*." St. Paul said, "Once you were darkness, but now you are light in the Lord; walk as children of light." The blind man, having received the physical healing, did not stop there. He found his *Lord*, as well as his *Savior*.

When good things happen it is a problem for some people, because the status quo has changed. Good news is a problem for those who are not ready to receive it. It remains a problem until we can begin to imagine another viewpoint—until we realize that "the Lord sees *not* as man sees."

To become healers we're going to have to offer ourselves to *be* healed. That means facing the darkness within. When we are willing to let God's light shine into all the dark corners, it's not going to stop within us. *We are to be children of light.* We are to become part of God's action. God's highway runs through *us*. Our job is to say, "Amen."

Sermon Fourteen
"The Depth of the Divine Mercy"
September 16, 1990 (Year A) Proper 19

The impact of the Gospel today is reduced by the fact that we don't know the system of coinage to which Jesus refers. One re-telling of the story puts it this way. A ruler called his servant to account for a debt of $647,000. But when he begged for mercy, the ruler relented. That servant then went out and found a fellow servant who owed him $27.42—and when *he* could not pay, had him thrown in debtor's prison. To put the story in these terms *begins* to make it more understandable to us—but *still* falls short. It's not a big enough contrast.

Ten thousand talents was a *huge* sum of money—more than the total annual taxes of *50 Roman provinces*. To make a comparison between the two debts: If the debt were paid in dimes, the smaller debt (100 denarii) could be carried in one pocket. The larger debt (10,000 talents) would require 8,600 people each carrying a 60-pound sack of dimes. If those people marched in a line with three feet intervals, the line would be five miles long. In terms of dollars it would be something like $10 million as against $25. Now here's the point. For an ordinary person—that is, someone who could not raise revenue by taxation or force of arms—ten thousand talents was an impossible debt for one person to owe another. One could *never* repay it. And that is the debt that each and every one of us owes to God.

Jesus tells the story about the two servants and their debts in response to a question from Peter: "Lord, how often shall my brother sin against me, and I forgive him?" As many as seven times?" That's the $25 debt—what we owe one another. But Jesus is pointing to the $10 million debt—what we owe God. To acknowledge the depth of the divine mercy towards *us* is to realize that we can set *no limits* on forgiving one another. Therefore, Jesus says, "I do not say to you *seven* times, but seventy times seven. In other words, we need to forgive as many times as necessary.

A preacher one time began his sermon this way. "Excuse me, I'm looking for someone, but I don't see that person *anywhere*. I'm looking for the person who does not need forgiveness, and that person is not here." Folks, we have a very large God. We are *unworthy* of such a God. Yet that God *cares* for each one of us and has called us into relationship, in Jesus Christ. This is a mystery and a miracle—and it's the *key* to what the Church is all about. It's about God's wonderful grace, or unmerited favor toward each one of us, and how we're going to *respond* to that. Now, if our God is so big-hearted—how can *we* be *small* in restricting or excluding our brothers and sisters from the experience of acceptance and forgiveness—just because their *doctrine* isn't quite right, for example? It's a matter of keeping things in proper proportion.

Some adults have great difficulty with the admission of young children to Holy Communion. Their thinking runs like this: "Is not the sacrament diminished, when the child does not understand it?" That is a Protestant view of the sacrament, which puts the emphasis on our appropriation by faith. The Catholic view is that God's grace over-rides our personal insufficiency, and the sacrament is efficacious—that is, it *works*—even though we cannot understand *how*.

To get back to the young children and the Eucharist: the difference between an adult's understanding and a child's understanding of the Eucharist, is like two ants debating who is taller while standing in the shadow of an elephant. It's a matter of proportion.

We have a radical Gospel, my friends. It's *dynamite*. We have scarcely *begun* to live into its implications. The Gospel doesn't depend on *our* worthiness. It depends on *God's* goodness and trustworthiness. We have a very *large* God, and *we are called to make him known*—through the life of the Church, which is the continuation of the life of Jesus. To grasp that is the key to understanding the Gospel we proclaim.

We depend *totally* on the mercy of God, which is the beginning, the end, and everything in between. *If we believe that*—how then shall we live? How can we *not* live lives of worship, and of service? But it all begins with God. And all *belongs* to God. And that, my friends, is the key.

Sermon Fifteen

"The Taste of the Gospel"

April 21, 1996 (Year A) Easter III

"Now that you have purified your souls by your obedience to the truth so that you have genuine mutual love, love one another deeply from the heart" (1 Peter 1:22 NRSV). This word of instruction to new converts which is our Epistle for today reflects upon the meaning of Christ's death and Resurrection. Truth and love are both to be seen in light of the Cross and the empty tomb. Truth and love are inextricably linked in any authentic proclamation or demonstration of the Christian Gospel.

Glendon Harris suggests an analogy from chemistry. Sodium is an active element that is never found naturally by itself: it always combines with another element. Chlorine, by itself, is a poisonous gas that contributes the pungent odor we find in bleach. When sodium and chloride are *combined*, though, the result is table salt—a flavoring and a preservative. Truth and love, says Harris, can be like chloride and sodium. Truth by itself can be offensive, sometimes even poisonous. Spoken without love, it can turn people away from the gospel. Love, on the other hand, without truth is flighty, sometimes blind, willing to combine with various doctrines. When truth and love are combined in an individual or church then we have what Jesus called 'the salt of the earth' . . . Peter said, "Now that you have purified your souls by your obedience to the truth so that you have genuine love, love one another deeply from the heart."

What is it that converts people? It is truth and love together: the two precious commodities that we need in order to trust—in order to give ourselves. We need the touch of caring that love provides; but we need also the clear vision supplied by truth, so that we are not deceived. A faith large enough for complex human beings is a faith that makes room for truth *and* for love.

How were the two disciples on the road to Emmaus converted, so that they recognized this stranger as their risen Lord? It was truth and love together—Word and Sacrament, if you will. First, Jesus *prepared* them to recognize him, by opening to them the Jewish scriptures; that is, he *reinterpreted* the prophecies, in order to show the disciples that suffering *was* part of God's plan for the Messiah. They had assumed that the suffering and death of Jesus meant that he could *not* be God's anointed one—the one who would save them from meaninglessness, death, and despair. The truth that Jesus unfolded—a profound insight into God's purposes—upset their preconceived ideas, but only to replace them with something better; an appreciation of God's intimate involvement with *all* of life—with pain and disappointment as part of God's total work of creating and redeeming and bringing to fulfillment.

Thursday evening, Nebraskans were shocked and saddened to hear the news of the untimely and violent death of Brook Berringer, an exemplary young man who for many of us had become part of our "extended" family." Besides the questions as to *how* this happened—trying to make sense of it *that* way—and empathizing with the pain of those closest to him—there came the questions, inevitably, as to *why* this happened. We were just beginning to come to terms with the death of Jessica Dubroff, the 7-year-old pilot, telling ourselves and one another that perhaps her death, which seemed so needless, could teach us something about priorities and perhaps not pushing our children so that *we* can live vicariously—when we were stunned with the death, closer to home, of a young man on the verge of fulfilling his dream of playing in the NFL. For both Jessica and Brook, life was just *beginning*. It seems so unfair—such a waste.

God doesn't give us the answers at such times; we have to work them out for ourselves in this life, and await the greater answer. But what God *has* given us through Jesus, the Word made flesh, and his teaching about how the whole biblical story fits together, is the Good News that God is *with* us in our sufferings and disappointments. They are not a *denial* of God's love. We have not been abandoned. Jesus died and rose again to show us that all life is of one piece, including our *dying*. All life, even death itself, is in God's hands. We are in God's hands at all times.

So Peter proclaims with boldness in his first sermon to the people of Jerusalem: "Let the entire house of Israel know with certainty that God has made him both Lord and Messiah, this Jesus whom you crucified." It is the *crucified* one who has been raised up and is now hailed as the Messiah. What was unexpected was not that God would *send* a Savior, but that the Messiah would *suffer*, and *die*, and yet be the *Son of God*. And the Good News for us is that *our* suffering and death are caught up in Jesus. Our anguished questions—which have no resounding answer this side of the grave—are caught up in Him whom God raised from the dead.

Jesus prepared those two disciples on the road to Emmaus by opening to them the Scriptures. But they did not recognize Him, until at table with them, he took bread, blessed and broke it, and gave it to them. Their simple table fellowship was transformed into a Eucharist, and their eyes were opened; they saw him as the host at *God's* table. And immediately he disappeared. They realized in this moment of sacrament—when God reached out and touched them in love—that they had been speaking and sharing with the Risen Christ.

It may have been that Jesus' actions at table gave them a clue as to his identity, but I think we have to say that it was God's touch that produced the revelation. It was the testimony of the Spirit in their hearts that suddenly put it all together for them, as they looked back and marveled at what had been unfolded, beginning with their conversation with this stranger on the road. They said to each other, "Were not our hearts burning within us while he was talking to us on the road, while he was opening the scriptures to us?"

Conversion, then, is a meeting of *head* and *heart*. It is not enough to have the *knowledge alone*. And yet the knowledge is *important*. But it is when Word and Sacrament *combine*—when truth and Love come together—that lives are changed. Truth by itself is not enough.

Elie Wiesel spoke last week about the seduction and danger of fanaticism—the overweening sense some groups or people have that they alone have the truth, and therefore the right or responsibility to impose that upon others, unchecked by love. Fanaticism becomes blind because it stops looking at the face of the other, so does not see there the face of a brother or sister—someone with equal dignity, and a truth that might complete our own. No, truth without love *can* be dangerous. But we need also the searchlight of a truth larger than our own, if we are to avoid fanaticism.

James Cutsinger, academic dean of Rose Hill College in Aiken, South Carolina, wrote the following, in answer to the question: "What is a liberal education?" He said:

Liberal education is education that liberates . . . such an education is meant to deliver us not only from our own passions and ignorance, but from slavish allegiance to the unexamined opinions of the world around us, especially current opinions that are often passed off as so evident and sacrosanct that it seems impious to question them. In this way, liberal education provides an antidote to the widespread disease of chronological snobbery—the unthinking presumption that the way things seem to us at the present moment in time is the way they really are. The liberally educated mind is the mind which has been freed for thoughtful reflection on the enduring and timeless questions of human existence.

As a postscript, I would add: those questions of human existence are the *very* questions we are asking in the aftermath of the deaths of Brook and Jessica.

The Gospel, or Good News, of Jesus Christ can relieve our anxiety; but it never leaves us comfortable with any smug satisfaction that we know everything there is to know about what God is doing in our lives. Rather, the gospel—that "table salt" which flavors and preserves us—is always calling us forward to new discovery and leading us into community where we can receive the truths others have to give us.

It is truth and love, working in partnership, that we see in the pattern of the early Church, as set forth in Acts, chapter 2. Of those early Christians, St. Luke wrote: "Day by day, as they spent much time together in the temple, they broke bread at home and ate their food with glad and generous hearts, praising God and having the goodwill of all the people." It was their sense of *thankfulness*, rooted in an understanding of the truth revealed to them in the death and Resurrection of Jesus, that issued in their generosity—their open-handed sharing of the gifts they had received.

So for us, the disciples of today, the call is to be "salty Christians"—to share with the world the flavor that comes when truth and love are combined under the Lordship of Jesus, the crucified and Risen One. Our call is to spread the Word, but also to be the *sacrament*—in our table salt, and in all our doings—so that others may touch and *taste* the Good News, and give the glory to God.

Sermon Sixteen
"The Deadly Game"
September 15, 1996 (Year A) Proper 19

My subject today is *anger*: the good, the bad, and the dangerous.

One of my resources is a chapter in a book by Dr. William Stafford, who happens to be my thesis advisor. Of course, we agreed some time ago that my knowing his thinking would be important to me. The book is ***Disordered Loves: Healing the Seven Deadly Sins***. And yes, anger *is* one of the seven. But it is, also, as Stafford points out, a very *natural* emotion. Anger is a natural response, whenever our being or essential activities are threatened.

We are able to live more or less peacefully in society because we have developed conventions for appropriate behavior. For example, if I am sitting in a restaurant eating a sandwich, I can be fairly sure that the person next to me will not grab it out of my hand. Society has provided sanctions—a kind of "corporate anger" directed at those who violate the conventions—so that I do not have to be constantly on the defensive. The problem is—and here I have many *other* sources—anger is far more widespread in our society today than would seem to be needed. Something is *wrong*, and anger is the symptom.

There is more going on than meets the eye when I encounter anger, whether it is my own, or that of someone else. Anger is more than a natural response to a serious threat. It has become a psychic defense against all manner of threats, whether real or perceived. Anger is widespread because it is convenient; it covers the motives we might not want to admit; and the exercise of anger can even be *fun*.

In his classic, ***Wishful Thinking: A Theological ABC***, Frederick Buechner has this to say about anger: "Of the Seven Deadly Sins, anger is possibly the most fun. To lick your wounds, to smack your lips over grievances long past, to roll over your tongue the prospect of bitter confrontations still to come, to savor to the last toothsome morsel both the pain you are given and the pain you are giving back—in many ways is a feast fit for a king. The chief drawback is that what you are wolfing down is yourself. The skeleton at the feast is you."

Buechner hunts at the danger. We'll get to that in more detail. But let's consider first the *deceptive* nature of anger. If you say something to me which I find hurtful, whether or not you intended it to be—or if you act toward me in a way that makes me feel belittled—I have essentially three choices: (1) I can keep quiet about it, and either forget it or remember it. (2) I can give you honest feedback that I was hurt by your remark or action. But if I do that, I am admitting to a feeling of weakness that reminds me of when I was small. And most people don't *like* to get in touch with that "not OK" feeling. So my third option—and this is really *tempting*—is to *cover* my hurt, my woundedness, my weakness, with righteous *anger*. Anger feels powerful. I'm *doing* something. I'm not helpless. I strike back at the one who hurt me. Yet that only compounds the problem. It may be that my angry response confuses you about what is going on. Or I put you on the defensive. In either case communication about the *source* of my distress is *not* enhanced.

Many of us use anger so much of the time in such a deceptive way: as a cover for hurt, for frustrations, for fear, for *guilt*—as for example, in a movie I recently saw, **The Brothers McMullen**, in which one brother is seduced into an extramarital affair. He covers his guilt with anger, whenever he is questioned. He becomes very irritable. He goes on the offensive, because he is feeling defensive.

Anger is *often* self-justifying and self-indulgent: it excuses various behaviors, and is a way of postponing what we know we *ought* to do. Anger is an outlet for frustration: a way of doing something rather than being stuck, feeling like a helpless victim. Yet anger is not always open in its expression. Some of the most angry people you or I have known are *passive* aggressive; they won't even *admit* to being angry. The anger is *there*, all right, but it comes out in sneaky ways, such as forgetting, or being late, or misunderstanding—or a host of other ways in which one can throw a monkey wrench into the works without being openly confrontive—without admitting one's feelings. Yes, anger is a *symptom* that something is *wrong*. But where is it wrong? That's not always so clear.

To be sure, anger can be appropriate, and even positive. Back to Stafford now. He says, "Anger that is right serves and protects something good. As long as the cosmos throws up rebellion against God's goodness, there will be a need for right wrath.... Social anger does not only protect one's self, or even blood kin, but the integrity of one's neighbor. It is right to defend a neighbor who is being mugged or a community that is being denied jobs or housing. Rage gives energy to ward away evil and to respond to injustice" (pp. 76–77).

I think you can see the possible danger here, too. It is easy to dress up our own hurt or frustration in the clothes of championing a social cause. It may be very hard to sort out, in practice, right anger, in ourselves or others, from that which is not so honest or directed to so noble a cause.

Another difficulty is: we're not very comfortable with the anger of others, particularly when it is aimed at least partly at *us*. We are not eager to hear much about the wrath of God, unless it is clearly directed at those other folks. So anger is often problematic, whether divine or human, but especially the human variety.

Our first reading today, from Ecclesiasticus, says that we are not to harbor anger—that is, hold *on* to it. The reason is that we all have need to *be* forgiven. How can we expect forgiveness, if we are not willing to forgive? Essentially the same point comes out in the Gospel today, in the parable Jesus tells Peter, after Peter asks how many times he must forgive another. These scriptures suggest that forgiveness is something we do for *ourselves*, as much as anyone else. It is a way we get free of the anger that is at first so attractive, but then, as any other addiction, turns on us and oppresses us.

Rabbi Harold Kushner, well-known author, tells of a conversation he had with a graduate student at the University of Wisconsin, who was doing research on the social dynamics of forgiveness. Kushner relates that what she had learned in her research was "that among all the people she interviewed, there was a unanimous agreement on one point. When they forgave someone, when they let go of a grievance they had been carrying for some time, there was for every single one of them a *physical* sense of relief, a feeling of having put down a burden. They didn't *realize* they were carrying this load of bitterness until it was taken away from them . . . they had at some level, been enjoying the bittersweet moral posture of being the aggrieved victim and hadn't wanted to give it up, and now suddenly they discovered it felt a whole lot better not to be a victim anymore."

Anger is deadly, both to ourselves and others, when we hold on to it. Anger bottled up turns into depression and deformity of self. It poisons our relationships. And it takes on a life of its own out of all proportion to our original experience of hurt, fear, frustration, or guilt. *We* are caught by it, more than anyone else. So this weird thing happens, as we say, in our anger: "I'll punish *you!*"—and find *ourselves* trapped in the victim role. The ultimate expression of such inverted anger, of course, is suicide: "I'll show *them!*" (There are other reasons, of course, why people kill themselves.)

Yes, we can hurt others with our anger. But we hurt ourselves most of all. Instead of getting the sympathy we want, we may in fact find that others are resentful of the wounds we inflict, passively or actively, in our unrelinquished anger. When someone commits suicide, we feel pain, to be sure, and we examine ourselves to ask how we might have *failed* this person—what we might have said or done differently. But *we* are also angry; we want to know *why* such a hurtful measure was employed, when there are better ways to cope with pain, and so many people who stand ready to help if asked.

There are things we can *do* with our anger, besides the ultimate thing we *need* to do, which is to offer it up to God. In the short run, anger can be *harnessed*. When anger is channeled, it can provide energy for doing good. Anger can inspire us to greater efforts. Athletic coaches know this, and use it many times to their advantage. The danger, of course, in *provoking* someone to anger is that we do not know, in many cases, how that person will respond. Instead of producing an energy that may be positively channeled, we crush the spirit. Or we could create a wound that festers, in ways I have already suggested.

Anger is natural and universal, as a human response to threat. It becomes a sin when we are overly threat-oriented, or when we hold on to anger and use it for selfish purposes. Here is what Bill Stafford says about the deadly sin of anger. "Anger is a sin against the sift of social life; anger has no neighbors, only enemies and obstacles. . ... In sinful anger, the 'irritable' response turns around a basically selfish set of assumptions about reality. The standard is set by our own determination of what is normal and right. Our own sense of self, the circumstances we consider important for maintaining that integrity, our autonomy of action, are going to be maintained no matter what. Deciding what is right is not left to God or to anyone else. . ... One basic expression of the deadly sin of anger is the effort to eliminate obstacles to one's self-definition and self-seeking. In this case, anyone who obstructs one's goals becomes simply a barrier to be removed . . ." (whether that is another racial or social group). In extreme form, anger takes the form of preemptive strikes, without waiting for provocation, as a way of maintaining our psychic security.

Yes, anger is sometimes useful, but it is *tricky*, and potentially deadly. It can so easily go wrong, and become a ravening beast that devours us. We need to look carefully and honestly at the *roots* of our anger, to discern what we are dealing with, or *refusing* to deal with, and what is, or is not, of God.

Anger may be an expression of love. It is more often a reflection of distorted *self*-love. God grant us all the courage of discernment, and the grace of forgiveness.

Sermon Seventeen
"Live in Love"
August 10, 1997 (Year B) Proper 14

I was taking the commuter train into New York City on Monday, May 5, coming in from the north, and one of the things I noticed, as buildings began to replace my unobstructed view of the Hudson, was the vacant lots. They were generally fenced in and generally full of trash. It struck me that there was no incentive to clean it up. It seemed strange that on the edge of a city where space is at such a premium, here was space totally wasted. An open area can be very attractive—a blessing to everyone. But here were areas in public view, at least from the train, yet privately owned, and totally neglected. A number of somebodies obviously didn't care. I think I want to ruminate on that some more, but for the moment let me just call it a graphic illustration of the exercise of human freedom.

We have spaces in our lives which we can beautify for the good or all, or leave neglected. It's a question of *incentive*, assuming we feel no obligation. Our first reading today suggests both incentive *and* obligation. Moses reminds the Israelites of their recent past, *and* of their awaited future. He tells them what God has done, providing for them throughout their sojourn in the wilderness, and where God is *leading* them, "into a good land," where they will have abundant food and drink. And Moses calls them to obedience—for their own good—that's the incentive. He says, "This entire commandment . . . you must diligently observe, so that you may live and increase, and go in and occupy the land that the Lord promised. . .."

The conference that I attended in NYC was Trinity Institute, an annual conference sponsored by Trinity Parish, Wall Street, as part of their outreach of education and ministry, their stewardship of the income on the land they own in Lower Manhattan. The theme of the Institute this year, the 300th anniversary of Trinity

Parish, was "Ordered Freedom: An Anglican Paradox." Fred Burnham, Director of the Institute, put it this way is his opening statement: "We Anglicans live in the gap between fundamentalism and relativism: between those who are certain they *know* the Truth, and those who are certain that there *isn't* any Truth." (I might say, parenthetically, that both fundamentalism and relativism are *well* represented in Lincoln,)

1997 happened to be not only the 300th anniversary of Trinity Parish, but the 1400th anniversary of the landing of Augustine at Canterbury, representing the reintroduction of Roman Christianity to Britain under Pope Gregory I, *and* the death of Columba, the Celtic missionary that same year.

Roman Christianity had had great success because of its penchant for order. Celtic Christianity, which thrived in the hinterlands during the barbarian invasions of Britain, and then showed great missionary vitality of its own, did not impose itself in fixed forms but lived on the dynamic of freedom. It was the *fusion* of the two strains—Roman order and Celtic freedom—that made Anglicanism what it was, centuries before the Reformation. Remember that St. Patrick, missionary to Ireland from Britain, did his work a century and a half *before* Augustine landed in England in 597.

Trinity Institute offered parallels in science to our creative synthesis in the Church's faith. John Polkinghorne, an English physicist turned theologian, told us that evolution depends upon the interplay of opposing tendencies. "Fruitfulness," he said, "lies at the edge of chaos, where 'clocks" and 'clouds' are interacting." There is an interplay in our world between reliability and novelty, between grace and free will. And the best place to *be*—that is, the most fruitful—is to be in the middle (the typical Anglican position) *between* two opposing tendencies or polarities. Quantum theory, Polkinghorne noted, is about complementarity: it is not *either/or* but *both/and*. Light, for example, behaves both as a wave and as a particle. Scientists have had to hold on to both sides of the truth. So, quantum theory emerged. And Christians should find quantum theory congenial, in light of our witness to Jesus, who we say is both "true God" and "true Man," just as we say that God is both transcendent and immanent.

George Carey, Archbishop of Canterbury, in his first address to the Institute, reviewed highlights of English church history and set forth three principles of an "ordered freedom" that can govern our common life, and which are characteristic of Anglicanism at its best. The first he calls a *theology of comprehensiveness*, which is not "woolly-headed" but which struggles to do justice to complexity and *all* sources of truth. Such a theology enables us to live with differences while not losing ourselves. He quoted Bishop Kenneth Cragg's statement: "In order to be hospitable, you have to have a "home." That's ordered freedom in a nutshell.

The second principle or characteristic of ordered freedom is *flexibility of approach*, according to the situation. That means we have a charter to use our God-given reason, even while we seek to remain faithful to our roots in Scripture and tradition. We have to pay attention to what is really happening to human beings. In this connection, Archbishop Carey paid tribute to our retiring Presiding Bishop, Edmund Browning, who was *not* present, citing his courage and his concern for the marginalized.

The third principle of ordered freedom is *collegiality* in Christian living and believing. Ordered freedom requires work, commitment, struggle; contrary to what many may think, it's *not* the easy way. Archbishop Carey challenged us in these words: "The more we disagree, the more we need to share with one another," in worship, friendship, and dialogue. And he concluded his address by saying that he rejoices to live in a Church that is large enough and rooted enough to be hospitable.

I'm going to shift away now from the Institute to two main characters in my summer reading. I was given a book this spring, *At Home in Mitford*—the first in a series of four by Jan Karon about a fictional Episcopal priest in the village of Mitford—Fr. Timothy Kavanagh. My brother then gave me book two in the series, and I got number three from the library. I thought Jan, an Episcopalian herself, captured a number of things pretty well about life in a small town and a small congregation—though of course, it was the love story that really *hooked* me. At the same time, I was reading a series of eight books by John Sandford, the "Prey" series (P-R-E-Y), featuring Detective Lucas Davenport, a hardened cop not averse to killing people who have made a hobby of it themselves.

I've been struck by the similarities, more than the differences, between these two leading characters, Fr. Tim and Lucas Davenport. Both are trying to make the world a better place, one by building a community of love, the other by tracking down serial killers who threaten the community. In their own way, both are shepherds. One binds up the wounded and seeks out the lost; the other goes after the wolves. It's interesting to note the personal parallels between these characters, who are created—I'm pretty sure—independently of each other. Both men hate to fly, and will do it only when they absolutely *have* to. Both have difficulty expressing their deepest feelings and committing to marriage. (Is that characteristic of males?) Both are generous, caring, willing to take risks for the sake of love, putting themselves in jeopardy for the benefit of another. Both men experience bouts of depression when they are separated from relationships and activities that energize them.

As Freud said, we need to love and we need to work. That's certainly true of these characters. They need challenge, they need reaffirmation, and they need someone to serve. Besides flying, Fr. Tim dreads big cities and the thought of retirement. What he loves is bringing out the best in people. And he loves Cynthia and his community in Mitford. Lucas Davenport dreads the drudgery of routine. He invents games as a hobby, then loses interest when it becomes a big business. He's an independent operator, but he likes to be part of the action; he loves the thrill of the chase, and the game of defeating a dangerous adversary.

What could these characters—who fear death and love life—suggest for us? Rowan Williams, Bishop of Monmouth in Wales and a video participant in Trinity Institute, said that our freedom has to do not simply with having choices, but with the ability to be what we were *created* to be. The question then becomes: what structures will allow true freedom to emerge? That freedom does not come without cost. We need partners, if we are to become who we are meant to be, and those partners, —God, friends, family, co-workers—have their *own* legitimate expectations. So our freedom, if it is going anywhere will *always* be ordered. We will always live under some kind of discipline, even though we may gladly choose it. As Anglicans, we are blessed with a great deal of freedom; yet we have structures, such as the liturgy and ordered ministry, which help to sustain it. It's important, I think, to see that the dynamic which drives ordered freedom—the incentive, if you will—is the life of God, and God's purpose for *our* lives.

We are called, as were the Israelites, to go in and occupy the land—a *good* land. But in order to do so, we live under restraint, just as God exercises self-restraint, in order to love us. Our epistle today urges us to "be imitators of God, as beloved children, and live in love, as Christ loved us and gave himself up for us. . .." It is love from which we have come; it is love that is where we are going; and it is love in action—our exercise of ordered freedom—that will most surely take us there. Love is more than what we *ought* to do. It is the very basis of our life and hope, of all that makes life rich and meaningful, whether in Mitford, or the Twin Cities, or whether we are cleaning up our act in Lincoln.

Sermon Eighteen

"Peace Within the Soul"

December 20, 1998 (Year A) Advent IV

And so we come to Advent V, and the reading from Isaiah 7: "Is it too little for you to weary mortals, that you weary my God also? Therefore the Lord himself will give you a sign. Look, the young woman is with child and shall bear a son, and shall name him Immanuel."

Ahaz wanted reassurance that his life and kingdom would be secure. But he would not ask for a sign of reassurance. Perhaps he was as *we* are at times: worrying and fretting, but not of a mind to pray. So God took the initiative. And the sign to which the prophet pointed is a sign for us as well, Immanuel, God *with* us.

Probably the yearning for peace that we feel most deeply— beyond our religious and political divisions, and our alienation from the physical world—is our yearning for peace within the soul—peace with God, in the center of our being, and manifested in *all* our relationships.

St. Augustine of Hippo, who was for so long a rebel against God, spoke his yearning for *all* of us when he wrote in his **Confessions**: "Thou, O Lord, hast made us for Thyself; and our hearts are restless, until they rest in Thee . . ." The restlessness within that leads to a restlessness in our outer lives is God-planted. There is a void in us which only God can fill. And since we cannot go forth and commandeer God, God must come to us. Our prayer for peace at this season, or *any* season, is a prayer not just for the ending of warfare, but for the coming into our lives of the Holy One: the Prince of Peace.

What are some evidences of our inner warfare and our need for peace? I will name three; I'm sure it's only a partial list.

One is the perennial battle between faith and doubt. On the one hand, this struggle is a sign that we are alive: still yearning, still searching, neither complacent nor hopeless. And doubt is also *honest*—as long as it is not an avoidance of decision or commitment. On the *other* hand, we long for the sign that would be so definitive that it would forever tilt the balance toward the side of faith. We have our moments when we feel all alone, when the silence of God seems to be mocking us. The Prince of Peace "has left the building."

We envy those, at such times, who seem so *sure* of God, who seem untroubled in their faith. We are *not* ready, however, to park our intellect in a warehouse somewhere; for that would be a betrayal, we sense, a breaking faith with the God who *must* be the God of Truth—a God much bigger than our petty human systems of conceiving God. And so we wait, and we struggle, to reconcile the signs of God's presence with the signs of God's absence.

A second inner warfare we experience is the tension between doing and being. Doing seems important, because it is a matter of faithfulness, of meeting the needs of people. And so in our doing we are always pressing toward closure, though seldom getting there. On the other side, being also seems important, because there is *another* kind of faithfulness: being true to ourselves, the God who made us, and to the significant people who need and deserve our more or less undivided attention, at least *once* in a while. While *doing* presses us to keep going, *being* insists that we need to stop and desist from doing, in order to listen, and to share the spirit of Immanuel, God *with* us. This may happen in solitude, or in one-on-one encounters.

Why can't we simply *stay* in being mode all the time? Because that would be self-indulgent; we would be neglecting many needs, neglecting many people, while focusing on our own needs, or those of a few. There is also *this* annoying fact: that the outer world will not sit still for long before demanding attention. The clock, which is *not* our friend, continually calls us back into the outer struggle, which produces the inner struggle.

No, we can never neglect for too long *either* doing or being, without doing harm to ourselves and to those we love. Yet striving for balance is not *easy*. Perhaps only Frank Sinatra was able to move effortlessly back and forth between doing and being: "Do-be-do-be-do . . ."

A third area of inner warfare is reflected in two opposing states of relationship, which can hold true either with regard to other people or with God, and often with both God and people at the same time. I'll call these two states alienation and connection. Alienation is what we experience when we've just had a fight with someone, *or* we realize that our values and beliefs are totally at odds with those of someone with whom we have been seeking a relationship, *or* when we feel judged and inadequate, perhaps excluded because we are different.

Alienation is not just what other people do to us, it is our *own* inner movement of despair, as we withdraw in spirit, if not in body, to lick our wounds and brood on our separation—our sense of not fitting in. With respect to God, alienation is when we don't want the relationship. We are angry with God. For those of you who saw Mimi Rogers in the film *The Rapture* a few years ago, alienation was her state at the end of the film, as she could not accept God's invitation. It's a terrible, scary place to be; yet one can feel paralyzed, unable to forgive, unable to move any closer, unable to accept the love which is offered. It takes a new act of grace, enabling us to let go of our bitterness and resentment, before we can be set free from that feeling, which is like being frozen inside a block of ice. Alienation is *hell* on earth.

So what is connection? I'll give a trivial example first—or maybe it's *not* so trivial—*you* decide. On my flight back to the U.S. after a one-year Army tour in Vietnam, I sat beside a young trooper who told me about one of his happiest memories of the preceding year. He had been lounging on his cot, drinking a warm beer. And suddenly he realized that he was at peace—he was actually *happy*—right there in a war zone, a long way from home. He was thankful for simple blessings: even a warm beer and just being alive. Was that a spiritual moment? Was it a moment of Immanuel, God *with* us—without the label?

I know some of my *own* moments of connection, with people and with God. In some cases they were moments of *re*connection: of once again being close to someone from whom I had been estranged—given a second chance to love and *be* loved. I have felt connected at times through letters, phone calls, unexpected reunions. I have caught up friendships that were dormant for years in a single visit.

I have felt connected with God in so *many* ways, so many times, it's hard to know where to begin. Strangely enough, not only are there days when I know I am moving in the flow of God's Spirit because things ae going so well, but I can also recall times when I was amazingly calm and at peace in the midst of a crisis, because at that time I *knew* I needed God's help—and I was aware that God was *there*; like the time I got the phone call that two children and an estranged husband in my congregation had been killed in a car accident, and would I please meet the state trooper in ten minutes at the wife and mother's house, as he broke the news to her. I also remember being *very* much at peace with God when the phone call came telling me my mother had just died. As I drove across town to be with my Dad, I was thankful that her prayer for release from years of suffering had been answered—that God was merciful.

The Collect for today, the Fourth Sunday of Advent, includes the petition that Jesus, at his coming, may find in us "a mansion prepared for himself." A "mansion" means *lots* of room. That means, for most of us, clearing some space—letting go of some things, including many *good* things. To be open to the coming of the Prince of Peace, in other words, is to be empty, and to know you're empty.

Perhaps it might be expressed in a prayer something like this:

"Lord Jesus, help me. I need you.
I need your peace that passes my understanding.
I need your love, which is unconditional.
I need your doing, when my own isn't enough.
I need your being, to make me connected again,
when I have been
separated, angry, and rebellious.
I need the gift of your presence, when I am unable to
reach out for you."

"O come, O come, Emmanuel,
and ransom captive Israel,
that mourns in lonely exile here
until the Son of God appear."

And *when* He appears, in your life and mine, then comes to pass the prophecy of Isaiah 40: "Speak tenderly to Jerusalem and cry to her that her warfare is ended . . ."

Amen, Come Lord Jesus!

Sermon Nineteen

"The Shepherd King"

January 21, 1999 (Year A) Christ the King

Before Jesus appeared on the earth, *God* was the Shepherd, says the prophet Ezekiel. And when the last vestige of rebellion against God has been done away, says Paul, God will *again* rule the flock. In the meantime, we have a Shepherd King after the pattern of David—a *Shepherd King*—who is Son of God and son of Mary. And we must decide how we will *respond* to such a ruler. Will we be *goats*, seizing what we can for ourselves? Or sheep who hear the *call* of the Shepherd, and the cry of brothers and sisters in distress? What does it mean to *have* a Shepherd? What does it mean to have a *King*?

Let's take the *Shepherd* part first. To be a sheep has to do with realizing our *dependence* on God. The notion of *being* dependent sits *uneasily* with us. It feels like a betrayal of our American ideal of *in*dependence and personal responsibility. But listen to an *extension* of the first reading we heard today, from Ezekiel 34, and see if it doesn't have a very familiar ring in terms of what is happening in America today.

> *"As for you, my flock, says the Lord God:*
> *Is it not enough for you to feed on the good pasture,*
> *but must you tread down with your feet the rest of*
> *your pasture?*
>
> *When you drink of the clear water,*
> *must you foul the rest with your feet?*
>
> *And must my sheep eat what you have trodden*
> *with your feet, and drink what you have fouled*
> *with your feet?*
>
> *Therefore, thus days the Lord God to them:*
> *I myself will judge between the fat sheep and the*
> *lean sheep.*

Because you pushed with the flank and shoulder, and butted at all the weak animals with your horns until you scattered them far and wide,

I will save my flock, and they shall no longer be ravaged . . .

I will set up over them one shepherd, my servant David, and he shall feed them: he shall feed them and be their shepherd . . ." (Ezek 34: 17–23)

In an early Laurel and Hardy movie, the setting was the trenches of WWI. The troops were about to go "over the top." But before they did, the captain designated one sentry to guard the trench—Private Stan Laurel. The infantry charge was successful, and the victorious American troops pushed on to the end of the war. However, nobody thought to go back and tell *Stanley*. Faithfully he continued to march his lonely picket. Years went by. Walking his post, he wore a rut so deep that only his helmet and bayonet were visible above ground. At mess time he would take a break and open a can of beans, tossing the empty can onto a *mountain* of cans that had accumulated. Finally, he was spotted and rescued by a low-flying pilot. It's a classic "lost sheep" episode. But the Shepherd is the one who *notices* who is missing and goes after the lost sheep. Of course, it should be added, that *some* sheep prefer to *stay* lost. And in *our* day, many sheep go looking for another *flock*, another pasture. However, that's getting *beyond* the story.

Madeline L'Engle, in her book **The Rock That Is Higher**, tells the true story about a party that was held in one of the big English country houses. After dinner, as was the custom at these parties, people entertained the company with songs, recitations, and other displays of talent. One year a famous actor was among the guests. When it came his turn to perform, he recited the 23rd Psalm, "The Lord is my shepherd, I shall not want." His rendition was magnificent, and there was much applause. At the end of the evening someone noticed a little old great aunt dozing in the corner.

She was deaf as a post and had missed most of what was going on, but she was urged to get up and recite something. So she stood up and in her quivery voice began, "The Lord is my shepherd . . ." and went on to the end of the psalm. When she was finished there were tears in many eyes. Later one of the guests approached the famous actor and said, "You recited that psalm superbly. So why were we so moved by that funny, little old lady?" He replied, "I know the psalm. She knew the shepherd."

Now my question is *this*: How does one come to *know* the Shepherd? Is it not at least partly through our having an experience where the Shepherd has come looking for *us*? When we are lost and lonely, left out of the party, we *need* a shepherd. And by the grace of God, we *have* one. The Shepherd is *also* the One who ministers not just to our *surface* hungers, but to our *deeper* hungers—including the hunger to be *known*, to be *accepted* (in all our *sheepishness*), to be *loved*, both for what we are, and for what we may *become*. So are we *really* as *in*dependent as the American myth would have us believe?

Now to the other side of the coin: what does it mean to have a *King*? —a *Lord*, as well as a *Savior*. At the risk of turning from preaching to meddling, I'm going to ask a question that one is more likely to hear in the Evangelical Churches. But it's a fair question. And the question is this: "Where is Jesus in *your* life?" Is he standing outside, waiting to be admitted? Is He inside the door, but just barely? Is He somewhere near the *center*? Or is He on the *throne* of your life?

Other people might make *judgments* about that, based on observing your *behavior*. But *you* are the only one who really *knows* to what degree Jesus is the *ruler* in your life. To *say* that Jesus is on the throne leads to *another* question: What does that *mean*? After all, one can be a fundamentalist, and still refuse to *love* as Christ commands. One can *say* that Jesus is on the throne, and be *deceiving* oneself. How do you *know* that Jesus is truly on the throne of your life?

The answer, I believe, is to be found in understanding that we have a Shepherd King. That is, we know that we *cannot* love, we cannot *give* anything, we cannot serve the *King*, unless we let the *Shepherd* care for us at every moment. We have no love to *give* unless it has first been poured into us. Make no mistake about it: the *sign* of Jesus' presence, the *sign* of Jesus' authority, the *sign* of Jesus' power, is *love*–seen most clearly on the cross. Where Jesus is on the throne, *love* rules—not control, not fear, not being *right*, but *caring* and *serving*. Remember that the *Shepherd* is also the sacrificial *Lamb*.

Jesus is the *Shepherd* King; and we who would be His *servants*, acknowledge Him by joyfully putting ourselves into the flow of His grace, allowing Him to love us, and responding to His *call* to love. It is not our works that get us into heaven; it is *heaven* that calls forth our *works*. And then it is not really us, but the work of the Spirit, the work of the Shepherd King in and *through* us.

The righteous—that is, those in the flow of God's Spirit—may not even realize what they have *done*. They will say to their Lord, "When *was* it that we saw you hungry and gave you food, or thirsty and gave you something to drink? And when *was* it that we saw you a stranger and welcomed you, or naked and gave you clothing? And when *was* it that we saw you sick or in prison and visited you?" And the King will answer, "Truly, I tell you, just as you did it to one of the least of these who are members of my family, you did it to *me*."

There is a flow in this world *away* from God—a flow generally dominated by fear and self-concern. And there is a flow *with* God—a flow of love. And language or outer appearance alone will not tell you which crest you are riding. So we have to *discern*. Then let us go with the flow of the Shepherd King.

Sermon Twenty

"A Spirituality of Work"

February 6, 2000 (Year B) Epiphany V

"For though I am *free* with respect to all, I have *made* myself a *slave* to all. . ... I do it all for the sake of the *gospel*, so that I may *share* in its blessings." In this passage from our Epistle today, St. Paul is sharing what it means to him to live in what he has called elsewhere "the glorious liberty of the children of God." He has been set *free* from the prison of self-justification; but because his brothers and sisters are *still* in bondage, he has chosen to go back into prison *with* them.

Can one be a slave and free at the same time? Rubin Carter thought so—as portrayed in the current film, **The Hurricane**. Thrown into prison for murders he did not commit, Rubin determined that *where* he was would not dictate *who* he was. The *system* said, "You are *guilty*, and we will *force* you to acknowledge that you *deserve* to be here.: Rubin *was* a victim, but he chose to *limit* his victimhood. He set his *own* schedule, his *own* agenda, for life within the prison. The paradox was: he was a *rebel*, and yet in many ways, he was a *model prisoner*.

Let us take this image now, of St. Paul and of Rubin Carter, both men free *internally*, though constrained by outside circumstances—one by choice, the other by chance—and apply this image to our participation in the *workplace*. What *defines* work, as against *play*? Is it not that work requires us to do many things that we do not *want* to do? We work for a variety of reasons; but chief among them, is to earn a living. We trade part of our freedom in order to meet the requirements of our work. But according to the example of St. Paul and Rubin Carter, perhaps there are opportunities for the exercise of freedom *within* the confines of our work. Perhaps we are more free than we have so far *realized*.

Here is a definition of work suggested by Greg Pierce, in a recent issue of **Faith at Work** magazine: "Work is all the efforts we exert (paid and unpaid) to make the world a little better place, a little closer to the way or reign of God. *Do you buy that*? Does *every* job contain that possibility? Or are some jobs *inevitably* a mixture of doing some things we *don't* see as making the world any better, as *well* as doing some things we *do* see as improving the world?

Let's consider now, alongside that definition of *work*, the definition that Greg Pierce offers of "*spirituality*." In his terms, "spirituality is a serious, long-term, disciplined attempt to align ourselves and our environment with transcendental reality, the ultimate meaning of existence, the holy, the divine, in a word, with *God*, and to *incarnate* that spirit in the world." Do you think very many people think of spirituality in these terms? Do people see it as a *call*, a *ministry*, rather than just a *belief* system? What Pierce is suggesting is that our understanding of authentic *spirituality* should drive and inform our approach to *work*.

Pierce suggests a few spiritual *disciplines* that we may bring to our work, and that many people *do* bring to their work. One is something you have perhaps never *thought* of as a *spiritual discipline*. That's the practice of surrounding yourself in your work, whether it is in an office or a *cubicle*, with "sacred *objects*." These could be pictures of family and friends, works of art, or items that hold for you a deep personal meaning. Most of us *have* these, *don't* we?

A second discipline Pierce suggests is learning to live with *imperfection*, both in ourselves and others. There are two values in this. First, recognizing our imperfections reminds us of our dependence on *God*. And second, it gives us the needed perspective that we have *other* responsibilities in our life, besides our *work*.

A third spiritual discipline we can bring to work, says Pierce, is the flip side of the second: that is, that we keep striving to *improve.* Acknowledging imperfection does *not* mean that we do not *learn* from our mistakes and strive to become better workers and better *people.*

A fourth discipline that we *know* is already practiced by many, as well as *neglected* by many, is the discipline of "giving thanks and congratulations"—not only for other people's *work*, but for who they *are*, and for other milestones in their lives, *beyond* their work. This discipline is not reserved for *supervisors*, it can be practiced by *anyone.*

The fifth discipline Pierce mentions is what he calls "deciding what is 'enough' and sticking to it." By that Pierce means not only challenging our *own* compulsiveness, but also challenging the practice in ourselves and others of rewarding someone who *meets* a challenge by simply giving them a *new* challenge—a new *quota*, a new *standard*, a new *message* that what they have done is *not* enough and will *never* be enough,

I think what we are talking about here is the "Golden Rule": "do unto others, as you would have them do unto you." The flip side of that is, "be as merciful to *yourself* as you are to others." It is important for *every* worker to have *hope*. And when we take that hope *away*, we have sinned against *God*, not just our fellow human being.

I think Pierce has the beginning of a good list. But his list is far from *complete.* I'm going to briefly mention a few *more* disciplines arising out of our spirituality—our relationship with God, our vision of ultimate reality—that we can bring to the world of work. This list will also be incomplete; I'm sure you can *add* to it.

One of these disciplines is *forgiving* ourselves and others, *letting go* of resentments and disappointments. Another is *reframing* the people around us: looking at them with new eyes, not just as *problems* for us, but as fellow children of God carrying their own secret burdens, their own woundedness, their own dreams. Perhaps we can develop an empathy for where they sit, greater than we have now.

Another discipline very germane to work, but grounded in our view of life and reality, is taking the *long* view. In simplest terms, this is strategic planning. A cartoon I clipped from the New Yorker magazine some time ago shows one dinosaur saying to another: "All I'm saying is, *now* is the time to develop the technology to deflect an asteroid." Long-range thinking shouldn't be the exclusive prerogative of top management.

Another discipline, that I believe is spiritually based is mutual *accountability*: holding *ourselves* accountable, as well as others; and taking the initiative to *participate* in setting the *terms* of that accountability.

Finally, I believe that it is a spiritual discipline to look in the workplace as anywhere *else* we are, to see what *God* is doing, where God is *leading*. Our *capacity* for such vision is grounded in our awareness of what St, Paul was trying to express in our Epistle today: that we have an identity and a destiny that transcends our circumstances and gives us a freedom to take a fresh *approach* to our circumstances.

This awareness of God's grace, God's Good News for us and for others, was wonderfully expressed by Bob Gambs, a retired *would-be* curmudgeon and former English professor living out near North Platte. Bob recently shared with a number of us by electronic means this poetic vision:

> *"Just beyond the very edge of everything*
> *which we are capable of discerning there flows a*
> *cascading river of joy which, if we are true and able,*
> *transports us onward to the place where the end*
> *becomes the beginning. To be true and able we only*
> *need to let go, to stop swimming against the current*
> *and let the river carry us where it will."*

That my friends, strange as it seems, is what it means to be at one and the same time, a slave to God, *and* truly free.

Sermon Twenty-One
"The Gift of Good Friday"
April 18, 2003 (Year B) Good Friday

Crucifixion is ugly—have no *doubt* about it. I will not torture *you* now with the details, but added to the *pain* was the *humiliation*—the exposing of bodily functions, the total *helplessness* of the victim. And this was *deliberate*. It was a means of *slow* execution designed to *shame* as well as to *punish*. How could we *repay* such a sacrifice?

In the film, **Saving Private Ryan**, a small squad of American soldiers in WWII France is sent to rescue the one surviving son of a family whose other sons have all been killed. The squad finds Private Ryan but encounters a large enemy force and takes heavy casualties. As the squad leader lies dying, he turns to Private Ryan and says, "*Earn* this."

Jesus doesn't ask us to do that. We *can't*. But what we *can* do is be good stewards—good *trustees*—of the gift we have received.

Theologian Robert Ochs points out that there are basically three ways we can respond to a gift: we can take it for *granted*; we can take it with *guilt*; or we can take it with *gratitude*. Let me guess that *all* of us have responded to the Cross, at one time or another, in *each* of these ways.

To *appreciate* a gift, I suppose, we look partly at the Giver, and also at what the gift *does* for us. What *does* the Cross do for us? *One* thing it does we might not at first *think* of as a gift. It's the gift of telling us the horrible *truth*—sort of like when someone points out that we have spilled *food* on ourselves. It's *not* much help when someone points out what we already *know*. Then we may feel they are *picking* on us, or lording it *over* us. But sometimes it's a *big* help to have something pointed out or explained to us, when we have *missed* it.

A company was attempting to begin a new pension plan, which required 100% participation. Every employee signed up except *one*. No amount of argument or persuasion could get this person to change his mind. Finally, the president of the company called this man into his office. The president said: "Here is a copy of the proposed pension plan and here is a pen; sign up, or you're fired." Immediately, the fellow picked up the pen and signed his name. The president then said, "I don't understand why you refused to sign until *now*. What was your *problem*?" The man replied, "You are the first person who *explained* it to me clearly."

Sometimes it takes a *jolt* to get our attention. And the Cross can *do* that. It has a way of slipping past our rationalizations. The Cross can tell us the truth that we might prefer *not* to hear, but really <u>need</u> to hear, about our need to grow in love for God and neighbor.

On the flip side, a second thing the Cross does for is to show us the extent of God's *grace*. Most of us have some difficulty believing that God really *cares*: that God could be *interested* in our petty problems and that we could be *worthy* of God's caring. There are many paintings of the crucifixion, some of them intriguing and imaginative. None is more so than the one that shows the three crosses and the agony on the face of Jesus. Behind the scene, the artist drew *another* face. It takes up the whole somber sky. The sky *itself* is one huge face—and the agony on *that* face is *greater* than the agony on the face of Jesus. Is God involved in our world? Yes, in the *macro*. Yes, in the *micro*. God is *intimately* involved with us.

Still another thing that the Cross does for us is that it shows us the way home, and so sets us free from the illusions and oppression of this world. In John Bunyan's classic, **Pilgrim's Progress**, the pilgrim is asked: "Do you see yonder wicket gate?" He answers, "No." But *then* he is asked: "Do you see yonder shining light?" He says, "*I think I do*." Then says the direction-giver: "Keep that light in your eye and go directly thereto, so shalt thou then see the Gate." The light we need to keep in *our* eye is the Cross of

Jesus, backlit by God's Love—the same light we see spilling out in all its brightness on Easter. We didn't *create* that light and we can't *earn* it. But we can keep our face fixed toward it.

Fulton Oursler said that we crucify *ourselves* between two thieves: *regret* for yesterday, and *fear* of tomorrow. It is the Cross of Jesus that finally sets us free from our guilt and regrets over the past and from our fear of the future.

If Jesus were only a good *man*, we might say, "Well, look what happens to those who try to do the right thing." But Jesus is *more* than a good man. He is the Son of God, come for *us*. He shows us where our *true* hope lies, thus relieving us of all *false* hope. The Cross of Jesus tells us the *truth*, *shows* us God's love, and gives us a *direction* for our journey in this life. That is *reason* for *gratitude*, which is a far *better* response on Good Friday than just feeling bad about the violent resistance of evil to the Light of Christ and the suffering that produced.

I'd like to close this reflection upon the Cross with a poem I have hanging on the wall in my office. It was written by Connie Backus-Yoder and speaks to our life journey—our "Pilgrim's Progress," if you will. We often get discouraged, when we see the gap between where we *are* and where we know God *wants* us to be. This poem is encouraging, and very much in the spirit of the Gift of Good Friday. It's called, "***Touch of the Father***" (1992)

> *"A shapeless lump of clay you seem to be, lying on the potter's wheel. You've been crushed, pounded, molded, and all of your grit and hard places gently caressed into one waiting, expectant mass.*
>
> *The potter knows your strengths, knows your elasticity and she knows your weaknesses and how you will hold together or not in the stress of being shaped and fired in the oven. She has in her mind the finished beauty that will be yours when all of the pain is over.*

She knows the time of trial and error and she may have to begin many times and maybe even rework you so that you are even more pliable and accepting of the good will she desires for you. You are willing to wait and you are patient in joy. You are aware of the hard spots, yet hope because you also know you can trust your Creator."

Sermon Twenty-Two

"A Family for All Time"

November 2, 2003 (Year B) All Saints Day

Today is a day of dedication, for the Lion and for ourselves. We celebrate today the addition of two new members, not just to our local church family, but to our greater Church family, the Communion of Saints. One of these new members is near the beginning of his life; one is in the fullness of life. As we welcome them, we recommit ourselves to the faith to which they are subscribed: the Good News of our Lord Jesus Christ as it is set forth by St. Mark and the other Evangelists.

What a great day it is to be baptized! What a great day it is to join the Communion of Saints, that community of love and prayer which leaps over the boundaries of space and time. This is a family that is always with us, even in those many moments when we are not consciously aware of it.

The Scriptures today direct us first to remember our spiritual ancestors: all those heroes and heroines of faith who may or may not have been recognized and celebrated in their time, but who have bequeathed to us the visible church family we enjoy today. Their faithfulness, their courage and sacrifices, are known to God; and we rejoice today that no act of love committed to God can ever be lost.

Next, the reading from Revelation directs us to that endless day which will not seem endless, because time will be done away, and we will live in God's eternal present, where love is all in all, and there is no need for tears.

Finally, The Gospel directs us to the present day, encouraging us to trust God and commit ourselves—rededicate ourselves— to the service of that which is good and true and lasting. The Beatitudes are about as counter-cultural as you can get. "Blessed are the meek" . . ." Blessed are the merciful" . . ." Blessed are you when people revile you and persecute you and utter all kinds of evil against you falsely on my account . . ."

The Community of Saints surrounds us, as we remember, as we anticipate, and as we pray and address the challenges of the day. We are never alone as Christians, no matter how alone we may sometimes feel. The people who have been important to us are *always with us*, because we are united in the Spirit.

This week we buried a man who might have been the son-in-law of our old friend and parishioner, Sheila Reiter. As I thought once again of Sheila, I opened the parish register which records funerals, and looked at some of the names recorded there—people who, not that long ago, were still among us here. I'll read some of the names that may be most familiar, starting with the most recent. Jim Purtzer, Emily Naish, Margaret McCallum, Laurie Fisher, Jerry Blassl, Alice Wright, Sheila Reiter, Margaret Blassl, Francis Cunningham, Mary Mahn, Bob Fahlberg, Margaret Krebsbach, Ted Kampman, Nadine Kingman, John Welch. I could go on, of course. Each of these names brings back memories.

Emily Naish used to sign off her letters to our family with these words: "Remember that God loves you, and I do too." Emily was always telling me to "stop and smell the roses."

Ted Kampman and I used to work together on the Nebraska Churchman, the monthly tabloid that predated the Nebraska Episcopalian. Ted was the book review editor, and used to join us when we did the monthly paste-up at the newspaper in Wymore, then had a good lunch afterward at the café. A finer Christian gentleman I never knew. Ted didn't have much in the way of worldly goods or status, but what he *did* have was *character*, and a fine sense of humor. I look forward to seeing him again; I'll ask him what he's been reading. Nadine Kingman was my mother-in-law: originally a ranch girl, then an Army wife, then a widow and matriarch. In her younger days, she was a bit of a wild thing. In the fullness of time, she was quite the hostess and activities director, winning for herself the family nickname of "The Supervisor." In her latter years, she acquired a refreshing humility, and I found in her a kindred spirit as fellow sports fan and celebrator of life.

Nadine lives on not only in her family, especially her daughter of the same name, but in the Communion of Saints, a portion of which I have had the privilege of knowing—and it is a rich assemblage indeed. Besides the list of names I read, there have been so many others who were part of my family or of the family here, or both in many cases.

It's time to stop rambling and bring this to a conclusion. The point is, my brother Rui, and my younger brother Zachary, you are joining a great family today: a family of saints in capital letters, and saints in lower case; a family of remembrance, and a family of anticipation; a family that the writer of Hebrews calls a "great cloud of witnesses." All these people are praying *with* you and praying *for* you. And as you face the perils and uncertainties of this life, they will always be with you, cheering you on until you cross the finish line, and receive "the wreath that never fades away."

Sermon Twenty-Three

"The Integrity of the Gospel"

April 18, 2007 Hastings College Chapel on the National Day of Silence

It occurred to me while driving out here this morning that there are two cardinal rules for a preacher. The first comes to me from Frederick Buechner, early in his book on preaching (***Telling the Truth: The Gospel as Tragedy, Comedy, and Fairy Tale***). He says up front, "Let the preacher tell the truth. That is important to me. The other rule I figured out myself: it's "try not to be boring."

Silence, when freely chosen, is beautiful and powerful. Like rests in music, it is the frame around our notes—around our words. Silence, when it is imposed, is *not* so beautiful. We are here today as an act of witness on behalf of our gay, lesbian, bisexual, and transgender brothers and sisters who have, for many years, been forced to be silent about who they are, and the injustices they have suffered.

We are here today as an act of witness to our belief, furthermore, that silencing a minority on grounds that they are less moral than the rest of us is untrue both to the facts and to the will of God as we understand it. We are here, therefore, in solidarity with the oppressed, and in solidarity with Jesus.

Julian of Norwich, a remarkable mystic and theologian, the first woman to write a book in the English language, wrote in her ***Revelations of Divine Love*** over six centuries ago that, "unless you love *all*, your love is not yet perfected."

The issue to which we call attention today is not only an issue for our society, it is a vital issue for the Church, because it is a matter of the integrity of the Gospel. It is a matter of whether we will follow Jesus, who said, "love your neighbor as yourself," or surrender to the prejudice of those who are governed by fear of what is different—what seems alien to them—just as men have often been reluctant to grant full rights to women, and white people have sought to keep other races in subjugation.

It's very hard to change the taboos that rule in a society—some of which, as those against incest and pedophilia, for example, continue to have a sound basis, for the protection of families and children. We have set many other taboos aside, such as presumptions about what women can't or shouldn't do. There are plenty of prohibitions in the Hebrew Bible that we no longer see as binding, such as the prohibition against high interest rates! But one taboo remains in force, which most people are unwilling to re-examine, though it badly needs to be exposed to the light of day—and that is the assumption that gay behavior is unnatural and wrong, or somehow a defect in God's creation, simply because it makes many of us uncomfortable.

It's hard to change tradition—though we have changed it before, and will change it again, on many other matters, such as ritual purity and church governance. It's always hard to admit that we have been *wrong*. So, for example, we perpetuate myths about American history, that are in denial of the facts about what we did to Native Americans, and to African Americans long after the Civil War. Not many people know, either, that we have had at least one gay President, James Buchanan. You *won't* find that information when you visit his historical home-site. We are addicted to some of our untruths. If you're going to break an addiction, though, the first step is honesty.

The Church has been in denial for a very long time—stalling any serious attempt to study the issue of gay people, and in the meantime, forcing LGBT people into the closet, doing violence to their souls, and to our own. The problem we need to address—and I've come to see this even more clearly in the nine months since my book came out—is not simply ignorance, but other factors that keep people closed to new knowledge, including apathy, discomfort, and the continuing mythology about gay people.

In going around to speak to many groups about this issue, I have found good news and bad news. The good news is that there isn't much overt hostility. The opposition many people feel is kept under wraps. The bad news is, there is still lots of passive resistance. A common response I have encountered goes something like this: "You might be right, but I don't want to get involved"—or "I consider myself a fair-minded person, but this is not a priority for me." Underneath those responses, I think, is the lingering thought: "Gay behavior still feels weird to me, so maybe those people are right who say it's immoral to be openly gay."

What makes the difference in getting people to take an active interest in this issue of injustice and denial of God's love for all people? The difference I have seen is what I call the "existential divide"; people cross the divide when they suddenly discover that they have a gay family member, or maybe a close friend—someone they can't write off or ignore. Parents generally want to protect their children, and many of them see the very existence of LGBT people as a threat. But when your own child is gay, suddenly it's a matter, for most parents, of protecting that child from what the society and the Church wants to do to him or her.

I think it's important for all of us who identify ourselves as Christians to stand up and say that much of what is being put forth by conservative church leaders in the Name of Jesus today is *counter* to what Jesus actually lived and taught. I'd like to quote from a passage near the end of Chapter 2 in my book, *A Theology of Gay and Lesbian Inclusion: Love Letters to the Church.*

> *"The Good News of Jesus Christ is love*
> *overcoming fear; it is not putting 'the fear of God'*
> *into people so that they can be more easily controlled.*
> *. .. (Jesus) often spoke in a confrontational way,*
> *but he left hearers free to make their own choices,*
> *honoring their dignity as moral agents. He preached*
> *a kingdom open to all, a kingdom built upon the*
> *power of love, not the love of power.*

"The opposition that Jesus encountered was mostly from people heavily invested in the status quo, people who were getting along just fine following the existing rules and power relationships. What grieved Jesus most was the spiritual blindness and lack of love he encountered, the inability of so many to put themselves into the place of an outsider. . .. He did not go out of his way to avoid those on the margins of society, but welcomed them and took their hungers seriously. He identified sin not so much in terms of outward observance, but as selfishness and smallness of spirit originating in the heart." (p. 22, Haworth Press, 2006)

I was a panelist back in October for a showing on the UNL campus of a documentary called *Fish Can't Fly*, which tracked a number of gay and lesbian people whom the evangelical churches had been trying to "heal" of their homosexuality. Several things were apparent in this account. First, none of these folks who embarked upon the attempt were successfully "converted" to heterosexuality. All manifested a hunger for God, however, and a hunger to find peace—or they would not have made the attempt to change. The remarkable thing I saw in the interviews with these people after they had concluded that they *could not* change, and instead had come to accept themselves as they were, was the creativity that was unleashed in them—and the beauty, and the peace—once they were released from fear and judgment. Their joy in self-acceptance was then extended into outreach toward others. Spirituality and sexuality—including being gay—are not incompatible. All of us are trying to become whole—to make all the parts of our life fit together. The piece that doesn't fit and cannot be integrated is homophobia—which for the gay person amounts to self-rejection and denial that one is a child of God.

Now I'd like to say something about what a healthy Gospel is, and what a healthy church looks like. Let's start with the Church's message, which we call the "Gospel" or "Good News" of Jesus.

There are two general views extant in Christian churches today. One is a view of God as so holy that *He* is offended by everything we do that goes against all the rules that have been laid down. This God is a God of wrath and judgment, who is only willing to accept us, His fallen creation (and then reluctantly, by a legal sleight-of-hand utilizing Jesus on the Cross as a substitute for the punishment that should be coming to *us*). We'd better be grateful that we have been saved from an eternity of torment! Does this sound like a God of love? Hardly! But it's a useful view, if you want to get people to shape up.

The other view of God is that God loves us in spite of all our failures, and sent Jesus to show us that we will not be abandoned, even when we have done our worst and failed to live up to God's hopes. The love of God in this view is expressed most memorably by St. Paul in 1 Cor. 13, and by Jesus in the Parable of the Prodigal Son (Luke 15). God's love knows no limits, even though we often turn our backs on God. It was on this campus, in the summer of 1976, as I recall, that I heard Agnes Sanford, in the context of a Christian family camp, describe God as a "fountain of life," whose very nature is to keep on giving generously.

O.K.—two views of God here, and you can find Bible verses to support each one. The question is, first, which one rings most true for you? —and which one is most life-giving? Which one gives you *hope*? The view of God you choose to live by will make a huge difference not only in how able you are to love yourself, but also in how willing you are to love your neighbor. Many people, sadly, have accepted a view of God which is *not* life-giving. The God they are trying to worship and serve is less loving than *they* are—a God who is far too *small*.

I've talked about what a healthy Gospel is like—a Gospel true to the love of God we know in Jesus. What about a healthy church? Here are some characteristics I would look for:

1. a community where you can be accepted for
   the things you cannot change about yourself,

such as skin color, social background, and sexual orientation;

2. a community of prayer, where the focus is on God, more than on any human leader;

3. a community that looks outward, to address needs in the community, and is more concerned with empowering the disadvantaged than getting tickets punched for the heavenly express;

4. and a community that reads the Bible with honesty and imagination, realizing that the authority of the Bible is the authority of God, speaking not only through the human authors of those 66 books, but also through people and situations today.

I was asked to offer some encouragement for our ongoing struggle for justice for LGBT people. There *are* signs of hope, which we can see perhaps most clearly as we look back. We've made quite a bit of progress in the past twenty years. More gay people are coming out, and they are coming out sooner—often in high school, which requires courage and support. There are fewer people now who will say, "I don't know any gay people." More churches around the country are beginning to take a stand for gay people and a more inclusive Gospel.

I'm proud of my own church, The Episcopal Church in the United States, for standing up against the bullies and bigots who are homophobic and proud of it—though they call it something much nicer.

Many people in the population at large are coming to be more accepting of LGBT people, especially in the wake of tragedies like the death of Matthew Shepard. The way change happens in society's view of gay people is through changing hearts, one person at a time. That takes place through personal relationships, through face-to-face dialogue and the sharing of personal stories, and through reading and sharing books that challenge the mythology about LGBT people.

Anti-gay mythology supports prejudice through the deliberate use by some, and the uncritical adoption by others, of "framing" language such as the following terms: "gay lifestyle" (which implies a choice, as against *orientation*); "special rights" or "the gay agenda" (in place of *human* rights and *equality*); "gay healing" or "reparative therapy" (which ignores the fact that while behavior may be changed, at least for a time, sexual orientation does *not* change; people who have a *choice* of orientation are *bisexual*); and "gay recruiting" (which suggests that gay people are more predatory than straight people). Worst of all is the use of the slur word, "immoral," applied to all gay behavior, ignoring the context and the reality of faithful same-sex relationships, about which the Bible is silent. The use of the word "immoral" trades upon fear and suspicion of those urges in others that seem unnatural to us; and it involves the misuse of the Bible, reading one's prejudice into the text.

It takes time to overcome generations of bad teaching, fear, and suspicion. But I'll make a prediction: twenty years from now, at least outside of the evangelical churches, it will be increasingly hard to scapegoat homosexuals for all the failures of our society; and a lot of people will be saying, as they look back at our time: "What was all that commotion about? How could prejudice against gays have been so widespread?"

Today is a Day of Silence—a day of solidarity with those who have *been* silenced. Tomorrow is a day to speak up—to be an advocate for LGBT people—to challenge the mythology embodied in unjust and inaccurate "framing" language and rooted in misuse of the Bible, and to be a witness to the Good News that God loves *all* people.

Sermon Twenty-Four

"The Pitfall of Familiarity"

July 5, 2009 (Year B) Pent: VI

Alexander Pope wrote: "A little learning is a *dangerous* thing . . ." To which T. H. Huxley added: "If a little knowledge is dangerous, where is the person who has so much as to be *out* of danger?"

Jesus came to his hometown. And the home folks thought they knew him. And he was not able to *do* much there. There is quite a contrast, isn't there, between the popular acclaim for David, in our first reading today, and the lack of recognition for Jesus, later to be called Son of David? Why did the people who thought they knew Jesus have so little respec*t* for him? Was it his humble beginnings? Was there a resentment that he had become too *"uppity"*? Is there a general human tendency to pigeonhole someone when we have a little knowledge, born of familiarity, so that we fail to see the depth in someone right in front of us? Maybe all of the above?

In the Epistle, St. Paul refrains from boasting about a mystical experience he had fourteen years previously, treating it as a gift, not something that made him any more special. Instead of boasting about his enlightenment, he puts the emphasis on the grace of God, which operates in spite of human weakness. Paul understands that it is spiritually deadly to have the spotlight on oneself, rather than on the mighty and mysterious workings of God. In effect, his message is: "If God can turn someone as bullheaded as *me* around, there is hope for everyone!"

Let's think a bit more about the lack of insight in those people in Nazareth who were offended by the seeming presumption of the local boy who came back to teach in their synagogue. Aesop, in his fable of *The Fox and the Lion*, pronounced this moral: "Familiarity breeds contempt." To which Mark Twain added: "And children!"

Why is this so? That familiarity breeds contempt? Is it simple ignorance? Is it the force of habit? Is it mental laziness, as we classify and dismiss? I'll give the nod to option C on that one, and offer this observation: it's awfully easy and tempting to let others do the thinking for us, whether they are news analysts or movie critics. Thinking for ourselves requires attention and effort. We have to *observe*, then draw conclusions. And always, we have to be on guard against ready assumptions.

I recently returned from an unaccompanied 1400-mile driving trip to Appleton, Wisconsin to attend a convention. Because of the distance, and knowing my limitations, I broke the driving into two days each way, and took advantage of the opportunity to stay with family. Even so, the driving was fatiguing enough. Along the way, I twice saw driver training vehicles. And like most drivers, I suspect, I was careful not to do anything that would surprise them or set a bad example—even though I knew they would be driving with the utmost care. I've come to think of driving as a kind of examination, every time out. It's like a pass / fail. Except the only passing grade is 100%. Over the course of 1400 miles there are a lot of items on the test. Now, as Perry Mason would say, "thank you for your indulgence, your Honor," here is where I connect it up. The biggest danger in driving, I would say, not counting the other drivers, is familiarity. Where do studies show that most accidents happen? Close to *home*. There are multiple reasons for that, of course, but surely one is the false sense of security born of familiar surroundings.

As I look back at my own driving history, I see that being in a hurry—as one often is when making a short trip—and carelessness in *backing* have been two of my common errors. When we're in familiar surroundings, we may be less likely to be observant, and less likely to question our assumptions.

In my old neighborhood, I tried to counteract that tendency by always looking *three* ways before backing out of my driveway: left, right, and directly across the street, where a neighbor could be backing out at the same time. That saved me more than once! Familiarity breeds carelessness—whether one is working with a car, or power tools, or high voltage, or dangerous animals, or young children with mobility.

Familiarity *also* breeds carelessness and superficiality in assessing the people who are right in front of us—many of whom may be God's messengers. People have a way of surprising us, jolting us out of our comfortable categories. Familiarity with certain passages from the Bible that we may think we know the meaning of, may deprive us of hearing a fresh word from the Lord.

Juan Arias wrote a book years ago, with a title that arrested my attention. It was called, ***I Don't Believe in the God You Don't Believe In***. In some ways, it's similar to H. G. Phillips' little book, ***Your God Is Too Small***. Both works challenge our habitual ways of thinking—or rather not thinking. Yes, we do need to challenge the assumptions of those inside and outside the Church, who think they have God all figured out. If people are rejecting the Church, let's make sure they know what the Church truly represents. If they still reject the Church, let's try to see that they are not doing so because *we* have failed, through our words and *actions*, to set forth a Gospel that is Good News.

We do fail, many times. We succeed with some persons, and not with others. Our failures may often be due to our not looking and listening enough, to the needs people are expressing, and the stories they have to tell. Our familiarity with Jesus, the Bible, prayer, and worship, and the everyday *people* in our lives, may dull our sensitivity to the *new* thing God is doing, and the new *response* that is called for.

On this Independence Day weekend, when we celebrate our associations, and our freedom as Americans, and also may be grieving for some things we have lost, it's an especially good time to think about what our citizenship means, and to notice the good things, the shortcomings around us—both those that are commonly acknowledged, and the warning signs and the possibilities for good that may be overlooked. God has given us eyes to see, minds to assess, and hearts to feel, if we will use them. Citizenship is so much more than voting. We are the stewards of God's ongoing creation, as we are the stewards of freedom and justice for all. God gave us the alertness, the courage, the wisdom, to think for ourselves, and to be faithful stewards of the Gospel, and of the people in our lives.

Sermon Twenty-Five

"Show No Partiality"

September 6, 2009— (Year B) Proper 18

Interestingly enough, a scripture not included in our readings today echoes and integrates them all: our first reading, from Proverbs— "those who are generous are blessed, for they share their bread with the poor"; our second reading, from James— "if you show partiality, you commit sin"; and our Gospel, from Mark, chapter 7— "even the dogs under the table eat the children's crumbs." The scripture that all these readings call to mind for me is from the 10th chapter of the Acts of the Apostles, where Peter, after he has had a vision showing God's approval of the Gentiles, now declares:

> *"I truly understand that God shows no partiality, but in every nation anyone who fears him and does what is right is acceptable to him."*

This was a big breakthrough for Peter; and it's a big breakthrough for *us. ARE WE THERE YET?* In the Gospel today, we see Jesus with the initial mindset that his ministry is primarily to the lost sheep of Israel. But when Gentiles come to Him, exhibiting need—and faith—He doesn't turn them away, but performs works of healing. How do we respond when people who are not like us, in religion or ethnic background, or whatever, appeal for *our* help? That is really the test of the genuineness of our faith, and of whether we are following Jesus, or simply the prejudices of our culture. For example, are we more open to people who are well-dressed, well-spoken, calm, and well-mannered? Are we more open to those who conform to our standards of what attitudes and behavior are acceptable than we are to those who challenge us? Do we "show no partiality," avoid pre-judging and stereotypes? Are we careful about assumptions, such as: "I have to do this.", or "I can never do this."? Note: In what follows, I'm preaching to *myself* too.

We had a very public example of partiality not very long ago that played out in the national news. I'm speaking of the incident in Cambridge, Massachusetts, where a prominent black professor returned home from a trip, found his house key wasn't working, and being tired and a bit impatient, forced his way in. A neighbor, being either A) alert and conscientious; or B) a bit of a busy-body, saw two black men on the porch breaking into the house and called police. This is all coming back to you, isn't it? It's sort of "old news" now. But can we still learn from it? How did you file that incident in your own store of memories? Was it an incident of racism, or an incident of police going a bit too far, or maybe a bit of both? As you may recall, when the police appeared, the professor produced identification showing that, indeed, he was not an intruder, but, in fact, the owner of that home. Why didn't the incident end there? Well, here was the problem. The professor, being tired and rather upset that the police were there, and that perhaps they weren't treating him with the respect he felt he was due, began complaining, rather loudly, that this probably wouldn't have happened, if he were a white man. And historically, he had a point. If we've been paying attention at all, we are aware that many African Americans have been pulled over by police for what the black community calls "DWB"—driving while *black*. Many young black men have been detained while walking down the street, on grounds of "suspicion." Racism? More than likely. But there is s further problem illustrated by what I'm calling "the Cambridge incident"—and that has to do with the psyche of police officers. Now I have shirttail relatives—three of them in fact—who are cops; perhaps some of you have police among your friends or relatives. Without belaboring this too much, I think it can be said that racial minorities are not the only ones in this country who are inclined to be a little bit paranoid. If you're a cop, there are times when people are glad to see you, and other times when they wish you would go away. Police often make regular folks—not just lawbreakers—a little bit uncomfortable. Clergy experience that, too. Showing up in uniform makes some people nervous—like they can't speak freely; they have to watch their language. Of course, clergy aren't going to arrest you if you mouth off. The assumption is, though: they might judge you.

Now with cops, there's another whole dimension, and that is what I'll call "the fear factor." Police are often called when people are *afraid*. But the fear factor I'm talking about is how *police* feel when they go into an unknown situation, such as a traffic stop, or a domestic disturbance, and where they may be genuinely at risk. They know there is always a danger that someone will react badly, and *maybe* pull a gun. Police are subjected to these risky situations all too frequently. Their heartbeat speeds up, their nerves may be a little on edge, they're hyper-alert.

How do police deal with "the fear factor," given that they want to do their job successfully, and go home to their families in one piece? My observation is: they cope with it by taking charge of every situation where they are involved. Because they are at risk, and they have a job to do, they assume—and perhaps rightly so—that they can demand cooperation and respect. If anyone doesn't cooperate in *every* respect—or decides to give them an earful—they're not inclined to put *up* with it. Police, because of the *fear* factor, and their *need* to maintain *control* of the situation, may or may *not* always be sympathetic and dispassionate.

Now back to the Cambridge incident. Was there right on both sides? Yes, I think so. The police were right to be there; the professor was right to think that, upon proving his innocence, the police should have withdrawn politely and promptly. Was there wrong on both sides? Yes, I think we'd have to say that, too. Each side, it appears, felt disrespected. When that happens, of course, the police are going to win; they feel they have to win, and they have the means to do so. When it all came out in the press, neither side came out looking particularly good. Have we learned anything, except how *touchy* we all are? I'm not so sure.

My point in dredging up this incident again is that we are called as Christians—quite apart from our particular job, or social standing, or sympathies—to show no partiality. Part of what that means is to use our imagination, and try to put ourselves in the position of the other person. What would it be like. . ..?

We are called to respect *all* persons, until they have shown that they are not to be trusted. We are to show no partiality—or to put it another way, to give people we don't know the "benefit of the doubt"—WHY? —because *God* shows no partiality; *Jesus* shows no partiality—and we are called to follow *Him*.

Sermon Twenty-Six

"Responding to Grace"

January 3, 2010 (Year C) Christmas II

There are two truths operating side-by-side in my life—perhaps in yours, too. One is Murphy's Law which I'm pretty sure you know by this time: "If anything *can* go wrong, it *will*." As far as I'm concerned, Murphy was a *genius*. But there is this other truth that I can't ignore: I see God's *grace* operating in my life, all the time. It's not enough to say, "Oh, here I was lucky—here I dodged a bullet." If I'm paying attention at all, good things are happening every day.

So how can these *both* be true?—that Murphy is a genius yet God's grace abounds. Well, it's a big, wide, wonderful world out there, even though there are a lot of selfish jerks using religion for their benefit, or disregarding it entirely, while they focus on greed and power. God has certainly not kept the world from becoming a very messy place, and in too *many* cases, a nasty one. But listen to these words from our Epistle today to get the big picture:

> *"Blessed be the God and Father of our Lord Jesus Christ, who has blessed us in Christ with every spiritual blessing . . . just as he chose us in Christ before the foundation of the world . . ."*
>
> *"He destined us for adoption as his children. . . ."*

If these words are *true*, then the good things that are happening in our lives are no accident. We were chosen by God, before we ever set foot in this fallen world. We are destined for good things, as members of God's family, before *we* ever did anything, or even made a choice. This is God's free gift to us, and it's pretty Good News.

I'd like to take a little time this morning to draw out an implication of these verses, and then consider the choices we do have. I have a Chinese granddaughter. She is a real gift to our family. My older daughter and her husband realized, after they had two boys, and before they learned they were going to have a third, that the genetics of his side of the family made it extremely unlikely that they would ever have a girl. Fortunately, this was before the folks in China realized that they might be running short of girls, to have wives for all the young, single men now growing up in China.

Cutting the story short, Paul and Laura went to China, near the conclusion of the process of adoption, and were matched up with a lively little girl, age 9 months, whom they named Elena, keeping her Chinese name of Min Xi as he middle name. Elena is now an active and verbal 5-year-old who has adapted very well to her home in America, including having three brothers. We hope that she will have a good life here. Will it be better than the life she might have had in China? There is really no way to say.

Any young person now growing up in America inherits all the challenges of economic insecurity which our society is facing, as well as the *blessings* of being an American. In some ways, China is better positioned for the coming century than we are, even with all the problems that country still faces. Elena is learning her native language, as well as English, and we trust that she will be able to adapt, and make good life choices, as she grows to maturity. Having a child at *any* time is a leap of faith, and we really do need to trust that God is involved in the process. Our children need more than any of us are able to provide.

So hear these words again: (God) "*destined* us for adoption as his children. . . ." That's all of us. God has one natural child, Jesus; the rest of us have all been brought into the family, because God loves us, and wants a good life for us. Because we are all children of adoption, brought into the family through baptism, we have a very large family; yet each one of us has a destiny, a unique place in that family. We have a destiny, and an inheritance.

Here is what the writer of Ephesians, probably one of Paul's disciples, has to say about that *gift* that we have received:

*"I pray that the God of our Lord Jesus Christ,
the Father of glory may give you a spirit of wisdom
and revelation as you come to know him, so that
with the eyes of your heart enlightened, you may
know what is the hope to which he has called you,
what are the riches of his glorious inheritance among
the saints, and what is the immeasurable greatness
of his power for us who believe."*

Who are the saints? They are our family—all those whose lives are dedicated to God, so that they *belong* to God, as *we* do. What is our hope? We are still learning about it, as we continue to learn the meaning of our baptism. Suffice it to say, though, that our hope is greater than we have yet realized—just as God's grace within us and all around us is greater than we have yet perceived.

It's easy to notice when things have gone wrong. What we need to be learning to see is all the little miracles in our lives—and more of the big ones. Each of us already has a story to tell—a story of faith—a story of risks attempted and obstacles encountered. Oh, we know all about Murphy's Law—how things go wrong when someone is careless, when we take one another for granted, when the universe on this particular day seems to be conspiring against us. But do we know the riches of our inheritance, and the power that is available to us who believe—who see the world in part at least, through the eyes of faith?

The recent storm we have all lived through has given us plenty of examples of both hardship and grace. Many of us no doubt experienced—in this time, or previously—the kindness of strangers, as well as discovered resources we didn't know we had. The question then, that our Epistle today presents to each of us is this: How shall we *respond* to the presence of God's grace in our lives? Shall we understand it, not as accidental, but as part of his eternal intention for us? Shall we choose to get to know better this Lord who has gifted us and continues to do so? Shall we begin to draw on the resources God has made available to us: the resource of our extended family of presence and prayer, and our heritage of the witness of those who have come before us? Shall we live in thankfulness, as people who are richly blessed so that we are ready in spirit to reach out to those who at this moment are less fortunate? Yes, there are choices to be made, even as there are blessings to be celebrated.

Lord, open our eyes to see what we have been given, even now in our brothers and sisters, in God's presence in our lives today, guiding us, empowering us, forgiving us, providing for us, so that we trust that when some doors are shut, other doors will be opened (and) so that we see that we have enough not only for ourselves, but also to share—enough strength, enough love, enough imagination, so that we all may truly come to know the greatness of our God.

Sermon Twenty-Seven

"A Change of Heart"

June 13, 2010 (Year C) Proper 6

Not very often do all the Sunday readings fit together so well, as they do today. Since it's baseball season, I'm going to start out in Left Field, with a question relating to our first reading, from the First Book of Kings. Here's the question: "What was the sin of Ahab?"

Notice that it was *Jezebel*, Ahab's wife, who set things in motion to ensure the downfall of Naboth, the owner of the vineyard. But it was Ahab in whose name the thing was done. And it was Ahab who coveted the vineyard which was the ancestral property of Naboth. Compounding the sin, Ahab sulked when his offer to buy or trade for the vineyard was refused. Jezebel saw that her husband was pouting and refusing to eat, and asked him why. At this point Ahab could have kept his covetousness to himself. He could have said, "It's O.K.—I'll get over it."—as most of us have to do when we don't get what we want. But Ahab was King. He was used to getting what he wanted. So he gave voice to his desire. And Jezebel—who had fewer scruples then he did—then engineered the plan by which Naboth was denounced and stoned to death, clearing the way for Ahab to get what he wanted.

What was the sin of Ahab? It was covetousness, violating the 10th commandment. But at a deeper level, his *heart* wasn't right with God. Instead of being grateful to God for putting him in a position of power and privilege, and treating that as a sacred trust, Ahab took it as a matter of *entitlement*, and wanted *more*. So are many persons today, who are in possession of great wealth and power. How much is *enough*? And who is *truly* on the throne of life? Being our *own* god is *soul*-consuming.

Now, let's look at the *Gospel* for today, the story in Luke 7 of the woman who washes and anoints the feet of our Lord. Note how Jesus contrasts her behavior with that of his host, Simon the Pharisee. Jesus says to Simon:

> "*Do you see this woman? I entered your house;* you *gave me no water for my feet, but* she *has bathed my feet with her* tears *and dried them with her* hair. *You gave me no kiss, but from the time I came in* she *has not* stopped *kissing my feet. You did not anoint my head with oil, but* she *has anointed my feet with* ointment."

And then Jesus adds *these* words:

> "*Therefore, I tell you, her sins. Which were* many, *have been* forgiven; *hence she has showed great* love. *But the one to whom* little *is forgiven,* loves *little."

Now I have a second question for you: From this vignette into the mind of Christ, what do you think God wants from us? Here is how I would answer: God wants us to have a thankful heart—a changed heart—out of which we love God and our neighbor.

Let's move on to the Epistle for today, which packs a lot of teaching into a short passage. Here are three of the principal statements St. Paul makes:

- First, "A person is justified (that is, made right with God) not by works of the law but through faith in Jesus Christ."
- Second: "I have been crucified with Christ; and it is no longer I who live but it Christ who lives in me."
- And third: "I do not nullify the grace of God, for if justification comes through the law, then Christ died for nothing."

Now I have a third question for you: What does it mean to be "justified" or "saved" and how does that happen? Well, based on the points Paul makes in the Epistle, we *cannot* save or justify ourselves. It is a gift from God, given through the self-offering of Jesus. All we can do is receive the gift, in trust and thanksgiving. But that is not the end of the matter. When we receive the gift, or as we receive the gift—because with most of us, I think, that reception at a conscious level is a process over time—as we receive the gift, our hearts are changed. What we do then—the works of love we perform—are evidence of what God has done. It is not our works that change God's heart, God's disposition toward us; it is the work of God in pronouncing us to be loved, that changes our hearts, so that we can finally say, with Paul, "it is no longer I who live, but it is Christ who lives in me."

Near the end of March, I saw a movie that was playing in Lincoln, called **Greenberg**, with Ben Stiller in the title role. Roger Greenberg was a man who, as I recall, was just turning 40, and he was a mess. His heart was not right, with God or with other people. He identified himself at one point in the movie as being OCD—that is, afflicted with Obsessive-Compulsive Disorder, a fairly common neurosis. Although there was no hint, so far as I could see, that he had full-blown Asperger's Syndrome, that's sort of how he behaved: that is, he was highly sensitive to the mistakes of others, and highly oblivious to his own. Without telling the whole story, suffice it to say that Roger Greenberg's need to be in *control* had hurt himself and others in the past; and now he was at risk of messing up a *good* thing that was happening in his life: a new relationship with a younger woman, played by Greta Gerwig, who had her *own* issues.

Greenberg's situation could be analyzed, I'm sure, solely in psychological terms; but when I go to the movies, I take my *theological* lenses with me. What Roger Greenberg didn't seem able or willing to see was the grace of God in his life, especially the people who cared about him, and went the extra mile for him.

When I say his heart wasn't right, as opposed to the workings of his perception and logic, I'm pointing to his deficient sense of gratitude for the good things and people in his life.

At the end of the movie, Greenberg isn't fixed; he still has a long way to go, to get out of his self-absorption and self-justification, and into a life of grace—a life of giving and receiving love. But there may be a hopeful sign or two.

For all of us, to be set free from the past and able to move into the future with a faith in God, and an openness to life, a fundamental change of heart may be needed. We need to be set free from the need to justify ourselves for all our sins and failures, set free to receive the love that is already offered to us, and to share that love with others. So here is a bit more of a response to the second part of that third question I posed: How are we "saved" or "justified"?

Based upon the scriptures for today, and everything I have learned through my *own* stumbling like Roger Greenberg—specifically, trying (in vain) to justify myself—I would say that God the Holy Spirit touches our hearts—often through the people in our lives and often through events, sometimes seemingly small things—to let us know that we are loved, and therefore, we are *lovable*—we do not have to justify ourselves; we are set free to love and be loved—to receive and to share, in gratitude, all the bountiful gifts of God, and supremely the gift of knowing our Lord Jesus—so that we can, like that first century woman who washed the feet of Jesus, both inwardly and outwardly express our great joy and confidence in the goodness of life and God's kind intention toward us. May God touch all our hearts, not just once, but many times, that we may grow in grace.

Sermon Twenty-Eight
"The First Requirement"
July 4, 2010 (Year C) Proper 9

It's been a challenging year, hasn't it? First, the winter that seemed would never end; then the ongoing rancor of politics; the oil eruption in the Gulf. . . . And we could all add our own personal items to the list. Even for those who seem to be doing very well, life has its challenges. So it is for countries and so it is for individuals.

So it was for Naaman, the commander of the army of the Arameans. The scripture says he was "a great man," and in high favor, because of military victory. He was "a mighty warrior"; but he also had leprosy. He didn't have access to the Internet, but he did have a young slave girl who provided a valuable tip, telling Naaman's wife about a prophet in northern Israel, who might be able to cure him. Naaman, being a desperate man, was willing to try almost anything. But being an *important* man, he took advantage of his relationship with the King of Aram, who sent a royal letter, along with costly gifts, to the King of Israel. That letter caused some consternation for the latter royal personage, who saw it as more an opportunity for failure, than an opportunity to build an alliance. When the prophet—Elisha—heard of his King's consternation, he was undisturbed, and said "Let him (Naaman) come to me."

Naaman was a desperate man, but also an important man, so when he came, with his entourage, to Elisha's house, and the prophet did not come out to meet him, but instead sent out a messenger with instructions, Naaman was offended and angry. He almost turned around and *left*. His servants had to persuade him to do what the prophet had commanded. Receiving the blessings of life, the blessings of God, is not always a matter of grasping and taking, or of striving and achieving, and receiving what seems to be one's due. Whether one is commander of an army, or CEO of a major corporation, or a person with a less exalted position, often the first requirement for receiving a blessing is to humble oneself—enough to ask for advice and help, and to listen to what one is told, and to do what is required. How much loss of stature and market share could have been averted for the Toyota Corporation, had its CEO been quicker to listen, and to admit fault. (I won't even mention BP. Oops.)

Jesus sent out seventy disciples ahead of him in pairs, as a field test of ministry, and gave them authority to proclaim the Kingdom of God, and to cure the sick. They went out and tried it, and were elated when they met with success. They got a little full of themselves when they came back to report, and said: "Lord, in *your* name even the *demons* submit to us!" Jesus tempered their enthusiasm somewhat, when he replied: "I have given you authority to tread on snakes and scorpions, and over all the power of the enemy; and nothing will hurt you. Nevertheless, do not rejoice at this, that the spirits *submit* to you, but rejoice that your names are written in heaven."

It's good to have a little authority; it helps to get things done. But authority conferred is rather different from authority inherent; and authority itself is only a means to doing what is needed. So authority, which tends to get all the attention when it is working, must step aside in the face of a great need, and a larger authority.

America has been and continues to be, a great country. Yet we have been, at times, a little too *full* of ourselves, imagining that all the blessings we have received have been a result of our own goodness or effort, or specialness. If we are to meet the challenges of the 21st century, and work in partnership with other nations to secure the blessings we need for our own people, it may be that the first requirement is for us to adopt a greater humility.

Now, what does it *mean* to be humble? Does it mean denying our gifts and abilities? No—just as, for an individual, humility does not mean putting oneself down, or confusing a *fault* with a *characteristic*. For some people, being loud, while others may judge it to be a fault, is more of a characteristic—it's just the way they are.

Wouldn't it be a better world, if we could all do these two things? First, stop judging others for their characteristics which we find annoying, and are tempted to label as faults. And second, look at ourselves and our own characteristics, take note of how others perceive them, and do what we can to open better lines of communication

Humility does not *mean*, then, labeling as faults things in ourselves or others that are simply *differences*. Humility means that we know where *true authority* for making judgments resides, and where the source of our *blessings* resides. That is true for individuals, and it is true for *nations*. What we need to be asking ourselves, as *individuals* is: What is God calling me, at this time, and in this place, to *do and be*? What ministries can I *alone* fulfill? What *help* will I need, and how can I be of help to others?

I can't *do everything that other people want me to do. Admitting that requires some humility. Nor am I exempt from listening to feedback and the earnest entreaties of others. I can't do everything; but I can do something.* What is it that God has equipped me and positioned me to do? And can I forgive myself, when I sometimes fail, through fatigue, or through fear? Can I forgive others, when *they* fail?

What is America called to do and to be? Are we still a land of opportunity for all? Are we a land of liberty and justice for all? Are we called, as Israel was, to be "a light unto the nations"? Do we have things, not only in our past history, but in our present conduct, such as our utilization of precious resources and care of the environment, for which we need to repent?

> *Again, "repentance," like "humility," is not primarily about feeling bad; it has more to do with the decisions we make, and the actions we undertake. It's not all about us, it's about God, and about all the other people on this planet, including*

those outside our borders. Do we believe that God loves the Arameans as much as the Israelites? Does God love the Arabs as much as the Christians?

Let us consider then some words of Paul in our Epistle today. (Gal. 6:1–16) Paul writes:

"Bear one another's burdens, and in this way you will fulfill *the law of Christ. For if those who are nothing think they* are *something, they* deceive *themselves. . . . May I never boast of anything except the cross of our Lord Jesus Christ, by which the world has been crucified to me, and I to the world."*

What is our authority today, as individuals and as a nation except the call of our *Lord*, and our fidelity, in humility, to that call? If the cross of Jesus is the sign of that call, how will we live out that sign? And how will God be glorified through our ministries undertaken in trust and thanksgiving, in response to the Source of all our blessings? May God bless this congregation, all authentic seekers of God's will, and We the People of America, on this day, and in the days to come.

Sermon Twenty-Nine

"The Power of Choice"

February 12, 2017 (Year B) Epiphany VI

To be human is to have the power of *choice*, and the *responsibility* of choice. We make lots of choices every day, some more or less without thinking. And some choices we agonize over. At those times, choice may seem to be a burden. The biggest choices we have to make concern our goals in life, and especially, what kind of people we want to be.

As I look back at some of the movies from this past year that have impacted me the most, all of them turned on choices made by the main characters, whether it was the young couple in *LaLa Land*, weighing vocation against relationship, or the conscientious objector in *Hacksaw Ridge*, or the hard-charging lobbyist in *Miss Sloane*, the choices made a big difference.

Choices are perhaps half of what our lives are about; the other half is grace. God can often help us redeem bad choices, and may give us a second chance to do the right thing. But our choices do matter, and we generally have to live with the consequences.

Moses says in our first reading today (speaking to the people of Israel):

> *". . . I have set before you life and* death,
> *blessings and curses. Choose* life *so that you and your*
> *descendants may* live *. . ."*

We have to choose and we do choose, and our choices matter. But, with one exception, which I will get to, our choices cannot finally save us. We cannot secure our lives, no matter how fearful or careful we may be. We do not save ourselves by doing everything right.

A good choice, in terms of becoming what we want to be, often involves risk, and is likely to involve giving up some other things. That is the choice, for example, when two people decide to become parents. Some sacrifices will inevitably have to be made, and we do not know in advance what these may be.

As we often learn the hard way, it is not only our actions, but also our words that matter. In a moment of anger or frustration, we may choose to say something that does lasting damage to a relationship. We may choose to lie, to protect ourselves in the short run, in the long run hurting ourselves, because we show ourselves not to be trustworthy. The truth, it seems, will nearly always finally come out.

We cannot have everything that we want, so we must make choices, based on our perception of what is most important. You will recall, I hope, that in the 22nd chapter of St. Matthew, a lawyer asks Jesus, "Teacher, which commandment in the law is the greatest?" And Jesus replies, "You shall love the Lord your God with all your heart, and with all your soul, and with all your mind. This is the greatest and first commandment. And a second is like it: You shall love your neighbor as yourself." Clearly, in the mind of Jesus, these two commandments are not in conflict, in the mind of God. To love God with your whole self is to be committed to what God wants. And God wants us to love our neighbor, as much as we love ourselves. That is neither simple nor easy, as the Gospel today reminds us. Jesus doesn't lower the bar of what is required. He *raises* the bar.

In the movie, *SILENCE*, which has been showing in Lincoln, a Jesuit priest, Fr. Ferreira, played by Andrew Garfield, is finally placed in a position where he has to make an agonizing choice: will he publicly renounce what he believes, in order to save the lives and prevent the further suffering of some other followers of Jesus, whose plight he can clearly see—or will he remain outwardly true to his calling, and by that choice, sacrifice those other people?

In that moment, I think, he understands what the apostate priest played by Liam Neeson, had faced—that priest of whom Fr. Ferreira had been highly critical, for failing to set a good example for the Christian converts in Japan. Fr. Ferreira had assumed that the most important thing was to remain outwardly faithful—to set a priestly example. But perhaps he had forgotten that the first of the seven deadly sins is pride, which is concerned with saving oneself.

Fr. Ferreira now has to weigh the crushing prospect of becoming outwardly apostate, that is, denying his faith, against the call of God to love these neighbors, at least as much as loving himself. That was the point in the movie where I saw the spiritual conflict. Yes, it is a story of suffering for what one believes. But it is *also* a story about difficult *choices*, and about *love*.

To borrow a line from a story I enjoy much more, Man of La Mancha, Fr. Ferreira was called to "march into hell"—his own *personal* hell—"for a heavenly cause."

The beginning of Psalm 119, which we read this morning, declares: "Happy are they whose way is blameless, who walk in the law of the Lord! Happy are they who observe his decrees and seek him with all their hearts!" Yes, happy are we, when we know clearly what God wants, and are able to do it. But I tell you, brethren and sistern, that in some of our hard choices, the right thing to do is not always crystal clear, and then we have to fall back on our faith in God, that is, our trust and dependence on God's *grace*, knowing that God loves us. For we cannot save ourselves, even if we do everything right. All we can do is commit ourselves to God, to love and trust God, and to follow the leading of God's Spirit in our hearts.

It is generally a joy to have the power of choice: it's what makes life interesting and meaningful even when our choice is how to react, when something bad happens. But our most important choice is always to choose the heart of God: that heart that calls us to love, with our whole being, the One who gives us life, and our neighbor as ourselves.

Sermon Thirty

"The Hope of Glory"

July 18, 2010 (Year C) Proper 11

The familiar vignette of Martha and Mary, waiting on Jesus has always seemed to me to be a story ahead of its time: a prophetic glimpse of a newer world, in which the roles of women and men are less well-defined, less rigid.

Martha was working hard to be a good hostess, and felt perfectly justified in calling her sister to task for not helping out—even to the point of enlisting Jesus, her guest, to help shame her sister. Jesus turned the tables on Martha, as he does so often, praising Mary for her ministry of listening, and suggesting that Martha would do well to follow her example. What was going on here? Surely it was more than a matter of challenging gender stereotypes, such as "women's place is in the kitchen."

Two millennia later, we see that gender roles have changed, and are continuing to change, and it is men who are more and more on the defensive. The feature article in the July / August issue of **The Atlantic** magazine has an arresting title, "The End of Men"—a bit of hyperbole there—and makes the case that women today, at least in our country, and increasingly in many others, are driving the decisions, from choosing the sex of their child, to holding the majority of jobs in our post-industrial society, and especially in 13 of the 15 job categories projected to grow the most over the next decade. While women remain disadvantaged in the areas of wages and child-care, as well as the proportion of CEOs, the author, *Hanna Rosin*, points out that women are *reshaping* office work, business leadership, and higher education, as well as many other areas. The question this raises, I suppose, is "How are men *dealing* with this change?" But that's a question for *another* time.

What I'd like to focus on today is the deeper meaning of "waiting on" a guest, and how it relates to the life and ministry of all of us. A book that helped me begin to understand this was Henri Nouwen's book, ***Reaching Out***, which appeared in 1975. The *subtitle* of Nouwen's book is: "The Three Movements of the Spiritual Life." (Nouwen liked to do everything in threes—like some preachers! The three movements he had in mind were:

> from *Loneliness* to *Solitude*,
> from *Hostility* to *Hospitality*,
> and from *Illusion* to *Prayer*

Just a word or two on the two movements we won't be considering today. Loneliness is a word with negative connotations, suggesting that we are cut off from fellowship with God and other people. Solitude is a condition where being outwardly alone could be something we embrace, something that feeds the soul and relieves our stress instead of creating more stress. Illusion, set in contrast to Prayer, suggests that our prayer life needs to be down to earth, and not a form of magic, where we seek to *manipulate* God or reality, in place of coming to terms with God and reality. I hope those asides are helpful. Now what about that other movement, from Hostility to Hospitality?

A visitor, suddenly showing up at your door, or even someone you're expecting—perhaps someone you know and love—makes certain implicit demands upon you as the host. It's not so much what the visitor says, but what is going on inside you. Are you nervous, because the house might not be clean enough, or the fare you can offer might not be pleasing enough? Is it the fact that your space is being invaded, and your time taken up, that makes you uncomfortable? Are you experiencing conflict because the work of hosting is diminishing your enjoyment of receiving a guest? Are you fearful of being judged and found wanting? Or is the real judge the one you have internalized? Raising questions like these is a way of suggesting that the prospect of any guest, whether a stranger, or a friend or family member, at some level may represent a threat, as well as a hope. Of course, you can't show that. You may not even consciously *admit* that.

And then, what do you do when the guest arrives? Do you see it as your responsibility as host to keep the guest occupied? To have a full schedule of activities? Or would you be willing, perhaps, to take some time off from the work of hosting, as Mary did to sit at the feet of your guest and listen—and find out what is going on with him or her? Perhaps you can see where this is going.

Nouwen wrote that we move from hostility to hospitality when we surrender our need to be in control, and put ourselves in a posture of waiting—not overwhelming the guest, but learning what the guest wants and needs. Nouwen defined authentic hospitality as providing a space where the guest can relax and be comfortable. In other words, the focus shifts from what you need in order to feel good about yourself, to what the guest needs to feel good about the experience.

The good news is, hospitality can be a win-win proposition. If what the guest says he needs most is a nap, and you allow that, then you have been a good host, and your understanding will be appreciated, and seen as good hospitality. To let go of the control, and move into a listening posture, is to move from hostility to hospitality.

One caveat I'll add here: adult guests may be better able than kids to articulate what they want and need. It certainly doesn't hurt to be prepared, as well as flexible. But your attitude as host is probably the most important thing. The two sisters in our Gospel reading today, Martha and Mary, are sometimes seen as archetypes of the active vs. the contemplative life. Jesus, then, might be understood as saying that "Mary has chosen the better part," meaning that being a contemplative is better than being a doer.

I think that would be a misreading of the Gospel. We need the ministry of both Martha and Mary, for others, and for ourselves. What do I mean by that?

It's a bit over-simple, but we can think of doing as giving, and being quiet and listening as receiving. It's over simple, because I have already suggested that listening can be a form of giving—especially the kind of listening that lets the speaker know that he or she is being heard. But let's assume for a moment that when we're listening—to a human being, or to God in prayer—we are receiving. We need that—even if it's only the television, as a respite after a day of striving. And then, yes, we also need to give; we need to share the blessings that we have received. The Christian life, lived in balance, is a perfect circle of receiving and giving. And as we receive, we also give. As we give, we also receive. Martha and Mary are the two sides of our life in this world.

The trick at any particular time is discernment. When do we need to put down our busyness, and just listen? That's where Martha missed the boat. And conversely, when do we need to leave our guest for a while, in order to attend to some needed preparation?

Those of you who have studied time management have probably heard this saying before: "The urgent is often the enemy of the important." The urgent—or the seemingly urgent, like the ringing of a telephone—seems like a summons to drop what we're doing—even a guest like Jesus, who may never be here again—in order to meet some demand, real or imagined. The urgent may be fear-driven, rather than love-driven. What if I miss this phone call? It could be something important. Yes, and it might not be. That's one reason, in our day and age, that we have answering machines—so that hardly anything essential is lost.

What we need is discernment—as in the question Alan Lakein always posed: "What is the best use of my time (or God's time) right now? Mary of Bethany made that answer without hesitation, and Jesus commended her for it.

We will ask and answer that question explicitly or implicitly, again and again in this life. And over time, by God's grace, we will strike a balance between the active and contemplative—as Jesus did in his ministry, when he went aside from the crowds from time to time, to pray or visit old friends like Martha and Mary.

When we're trying to find a way to regain our balance, the Epistle today reminds us that Jesus is that way. "All things have been created through him and for him. He himself is before all things, and *in him all things hold together....*" Then St, Paul adds this coda: "the mystery that has been hidden throughout the ages ... has now been revealed to his saints. To them God chose to make known how great among the Gentiles are the riches of the glory of this mystery, which is Christ *in you*, the hope of glory."

Sermon Thirty-One
"What's the Point?""
August 1, 2010 (Year C) Proper 153

I'm here this morning because of a *death*—one of those all-too-human eventualities that brings us up short, and reminds us that life is precious, and not to be wasted. A death may be the occasion for our reflection about what is truly important in life. When things are just mudding along, we could be tempted to ask, as was the writer of Ecclesiastes, "What's the *point*?" What's the point of all our striving—our accumulation of wealth, our collection of things, even our achievements, and our service? Someone else will take possession of what we own, or have contributed, and may not even value it. Death gives the lie to our imagining that our fate is in our own hands. All of our work may then be viewed as having been done for nothing. "All is vanity," says the writer, supposedly Solomon.

Well, it's not quite that bad. People do remember—at least for a while—our good works—especially those good deeds we did simply because they were right and needed, and not to win approval. People often get respect for having accumulated a lot of wealth—depending on how they did it. But, at the end, you're not around to enjoy it or control it—that's the thing. So what's the point of our lives, if it's not simply what we leave behind for others to enjoy?

Certainly, the accumulation of wealth is not a sufficient justification for the investment of our lives—as the Gospel for today makes clear. The parable Jesus tells concerns a rich man who is worried, because his store of grain and goods is overflowing. Death brings him up short. Strangely enough, death wasn't something he had factored into his plans. So we called him a rich fool—and we see him as poor—in values, and in insight.

The frame around the parable is someone trying to enlist Jesus in helping him secure a share of his family inheritance. It might have been a just claim, but Jesus warns him against the blindness associated with covetousness, and tells a parable to drive home the point. "One's life does not consist in the abundance of possessions," Jesus says. Abundance may be a means of keeping score, but finally, it doesn't matter. So what *is* our life about? What's the *real* point?

The Psalm selected for today—a portion of Psalm 49—has two verses in it that I have long found to be one of the most arresting passages in the entire Bible. Verses 6 and 7 declare: "We can never ransom ourselves, or deliver to God the price of our life; For the ransom of our life is so great that we should never have enough to pay it . . ." These verses appear right after the verses that say, in effect: Why should I be afraid of those who put their trust in wealth? And the verses come right before verse 8, which exposes as fantasy the notion that maybe—just maybe—if we did have enough wealth, we could pay off God, and not owe him a death!

Verses 6 and 7 declare that what we owe to God for our lives is immense. Just think of that for a moment. Our lives are precious. We are precious. Yet we do not belong to ourselves. St. Paul says the same thing in 1 Cor. 6, and repeats it in 1 Cor. 7: "you were brought with a price; therefore glorify God in your body." (6:20) "You were bought with a price; do not become slaves to human masters." (7:23) We know that the price of our life and freedom and much more besides, was paid by the free offering of our brother and Lord, Jesus. And in the Epistle today, Paul says: "Set your minds on things that are above, not on things that are on earth, for you have died, and your life is hidden with Christ in God." (Col. 3:2)

A death changes everything. This death gives us life; but at the same time, it means that we are joined with Christ, in His death, as well as in His risen life. This is the answer to those who are asking, on the one hand, "What's the point of life, and all of our striving"—when we're only going to die? And it's the answer, on the other hand, to those who are so caught up in the petty rivalries and jealousies of life, such as whether they're going to need bigger barns to store everything, that they have lost sight of how short and *precious* life is. The point is that we do not belong to ourselves. We belong to God, and our lives and destinies are hidden with God in Christ.

That's bad news to human greed and hubris; it's good news to those who wonder, "Am I really loved? Is my life really worth anything?" Yes, your life is precious: it's worth more than anything you could ever do, any price you could ever pay. So now the question becomes: "What shall I do with this precious life, which I do not own, but of which I am the steward, or manager?" As the saying goes: "Now we're getting someplace!"

Nearly thirty years ago, a man named Alan Lakein wrote a little book entitled, ***How to Get Control of Your Time and Your Life***. The title could be misleading, because as we have just reviewed, it's not "our" time and "our" life. We belong to God. And the point for Christians isn't even about getting control. But this is a very useful book for managers—which is what we are. The question Lakein urges to ask, over and over in our lives, is this: "What is the best use of (my) time [or God's time] right now?"

As we may read a bit further on in the Book of Ecclesiastes, in Chapter 9, sometimes the answer to Lakein's question, once we have seen that death comes to all of us, rich and poor, foolish and wise, righteous and wicked—sometimes the answer to the question, "What is the best use of (the) time right now?" is" "Go eat your bread with enjoyment, and drink your wine with a merry heart. . . . Enjoy life with the wife whom you love . . . (and) whatever your hand finds to do, do with your might . . ."

At other times—for Ecclesiastes reminds us (in Chapter 3) that there are other times—"For everything there is a season . . . a time to be born, and a time to die . . . A time to mourn, and a time to dance . . ." (Eccles. 3:1–8) So at another time the answer to Lakein's question may be: Repent—change your mind, and your direction; go and make peace with your neighbor, while there is time.

"What is the best use of (my) time right now?" That's always a good question to ask, and Lakein gives some guidance to help us sort out the priorities:

> *Priority A*—our bread and butter: What do we need to do to make a living and take care of our families?
>
> *Priority B*—what are the things that make our lives meaningful and worthwhile?—things that bring joy to ourselves and others?
>
> *Priority C*—all things that other people try to make us feel guilty about—all the shoulds—"I really should do this, but I don't want to, and essentially I don't have to."

Lakein advises us, that it's O.K. to postpone the Priority C's until they expire or until they *become* A's or B's. don't allow them to crowd out the A's and B's. Death is coming soon enough.

Lakein and his question are helpful, but not as helpful as knowing to whom we belong, and how precious our lives are. May God strengthen that awareness in all of us, now and in the days to come. Amen.

Sermon Thirty-Two

"What Faith Requires""

August 15, 2010 (Year C) Proper 15

Having a living faith in the Blessed Trinity, Father, Son, and Holy Spirit, is a blessing. As with every other gift in life though, whether a pet or your health, faith requires some maintenance or care. Faith, any more than a warm puppy, isn't a gift you can keep alive by putting it on a shelf in the closet and closing the door. Faith is kept alive and healthy by *exercising* it. It's like a *muscle* that way: use it or lose it.

So that's part of the bad news, if you haven't been doing much to keep your faith alive. Now, here's the *worse* news. If you are using your faith—e.g. in the decisions you make, and what you stand up for—you won't be able to avoid conflict. Many people hope the Church will be a *refuge* from conflict—and would like to see it operate that way. But the Church is in business not to *shield* people from the world, the flesh, and the devil, but to equip them to stand up to the world, the flesh, and the devil.

Keep in mind that when we speak in Biblical terms about "the flesh," we're not speaking of the body; rather, we are using the term "flesh" as St. Paul used it—the Greek word is *sarx*—to describe an attitude of *opposition* to God, with overtones of self-centeredness and idolatry—not a healthy celebration of the good gifts of creation, including our bodies. The Bible makes clear, in the first three chapters of Genesis that everything God has created is good. It is only when human beings, in their contrariness, put their wills in opposition to God's will, that the world becomes a fallen place, and God's good gifts are corrupted.

So the Church, as I was saying, is not in the business of *protecting* us from life, but rather *equipping* us to live lives of courage and faithfulness in this world. Conflict comes along for many reasons, not the least of which is sin. Conflict also arises from ignorance and inattention, and misperception, and from *willing* ignorance (which is a sin), and from the *lies* that people tell in order to avoid responsibility, and to get their own way. As long as there are people in the world—people who have not yet been perfected in love (which includes nearly all of us)—there will be conflict.

Our readings this morning call attention to the presence of conflict, both in the secular life, and in our journeys of faith. Jesus in the Gospel says, "I came to bring *fire* to the earth. . . ." Not fire in the sense of final judgment, but fire as the light of *truth*—exposing the lies, and forcing people to choose where they will stand. Such choices bring division, even in families.

Now, is that wrong of Jesus? If we prefer not to have conflict, and would rather have "gentle Jesus, meek and mild," who keeps God's truth to Himself, we might say so. If we want Jesus the Christ, Son of the Living God, who manifests in His own being the Spirit of God, then we have to allow Him to burn in His witness to *perfect Love*, and the truth which *purifies*, as precious metal is purified in the fire.

Oh, there are plenty of *fire and brimstone* preachers out there who love to talk about the fire—the fire which destroys all of God's *enemies*—which includes everyone those preachers *disagree* with. I don't believe they're talking about the same fire! *Their* fire would burn *library books* of which they disapprove. *Their* fire, which is a fire of *fear*, has *already* burned uppity *women*, who were accused of being *witches*. The fire and brimstone preachers would set us on a *new* witch hunt today, against anyone who espouses a different faith, or who isn't an American citizen, or who doesn't read the Bible as they do. That's not the kind of fire Jesus was talking about. Jesus was talking about opposition to the will of God, that we should love our neighbors as ourselves, and should rid ourselves of the hypocrisy that says one thing and does another, extolling freedom for ourselves while denying it to others.

The *fear*-based fire made martyrs out of many of our spiritual ancestors—as described in our Epistle today. They were stoned to death, they were sawn in two, they were killed by the sword . . ."They went about . . . destitute, persecuted, tormented—of whom the world was not worthy."

Will we avoid their fate? Well, hopefully the worst of it. But we won't avoid the necessity—if we want to have a living faith—of standing up for what we believe—and I don't mean our personal preferences. If we don't want to be around people who are not like us, we're missing the point. If we think we can smother conflict, we're kidding ourselves. Conflicts denied are conflicts perpetuated, whether in a community, or in a family.

The truth that appeared in the person of Jesus is a truth that takes up the cause of those who *have* no one else to take up their cause. It is a truth that says there can be no real and lasting peace without *justice*. So is *that* the truth to which *we* are committed? We have to *choose*.

Our commitments, as Jesus indicated, affect our relationships. Our commitments mean that others who are close to us will also pay a price. That's true if you decide to serve in uniform in the service of your country, or if your kids want to take up sports or a musical instrument. And if you're unlucky enough to have a full-blown saint in your family—someone who hears God speaking and feels the force of moral necessity to help the needy, for example—you will suffer right along with that person.

St. Teresa of Lisieux was the youngest child in her large family—a family that was not wealthy—but because she was devoted to prayer, she needed to have her own room. What a pain that was. In our own day, Mother Teresa of Calcutta, and Mahatma Gandhi made demands on themselves, in their service to God, that greatly inconvenienced those closest to them. So if you're throwing in your lot with Jesus—not just one of his noisy faux-friends—if that's the choice you've made, *expect* to be inconvenienced. Expect to have disagreements, even in your own family. That's what your faith—your living faith—is going to require.

Here's a little more bad news, if you can stand it. If you want peace—*real* peace that is more than *conflict* papered *over*—it's going to *cost* you. Peace as our ultimate aim brings conflict in the short run—e.g., enforcing discipline with young people, or intervening with an alcoholic. If we want peace for the people of Mexico, instead of the increasing domination and savagery of the drug cartels, we're going to have to do something about the drug habit that so many Americans have, that is a big fuel to the cartels. If we want to reduce our involvement in foreign wars, we're going to have to reduce our dependence on foreign oil, and start getting serious about alternative energy sources. Yes, it is our choices today—some of which involve making changes in our way of living, and dealing with the inevitable conflicts that will determine whether we have a more peaceful and more prosperous future.

Now, I've tried to be true to our Scriptures today, which seem to present more bad news than good news. So here's the *Good News:* The saints of old did not live to see the fulfillment of all their hopes. Nor will we. But they had something infinitely precious—a living faith that sustained them in all their travails and gave them conviction that their sufferings and their witness were not in vain. We have that same gift: the gift of faith in a God who remains faithful, even when many people do not remain faithful. Choose Jesus and His Fire of Love, and you will find joy to sustain you.

And here's *more* Good News. We do not pray and struggle alone. For here on the earth, and in the realm beyond space and time, we are surrounded by a great cloud of witnesses we cannot see, who are praying for us, even as we pray for them. May God give us the vision of a vast community of Love—a community that has been through the purifying fire, and now enjoys the reward of faith—seeing our God face-to-face.

Sermon Thirty-Three

"Where Do We Put Our Faith""

October 24, 2010 (Year C) Proper 25

Over the years, most of us have had the Christian faith presented to us a number of times, as if brand new, by various eager advocates: eager, because they wanted to establish their bonafides, or, because they were concerned that we might not yet have truly embraced it, or, because they wanted us to act in ways appropriate to the faith they embraced!

Some of these presentations we found appealing; others we did not.

The question I would raise for you this morning is this: Where exactly did they want you to invest your faith?

- In the words of the Bible quoted to you?
- In the earnestness and winsomeness of their presentation?
- In the decisions and actions you might make in response?
- Or in the character of the God they were representing to you?

Among these choices, I would pick "D"—that is, God revealed to us by Jesus. But alas, most of the presentations I have heard in my short lifetime focused on one of the other alternatives. Either the bare words of Holy Writ were supposed to sell it, and invite my response. Or I was supposed to be moved by the presenter's sincerity and devotion. Or I was supposed to do something which would be decisive in governing my future relationship with God.

I submit to you, on the basis of our readings today, and on the Church's historical and Biblical tradition, and upon the exercise of our own God-given powers of reason in reflecting on our experience, that we must put our faith in the character of God, and nowhere else. Let's begin with the Gospel passage for today, this familiar vignette of the Pharisee and the tax collector, or as the official was called in the King James Version, the *Publican*. This parable of Jesus is introduced with a side comment by Luke, or one of his scribes, that is illuminating, namely: "Jesus told this parable to some who trusted in themselves that they were righteous and regarded others with contempt." Normally we expect to hear a parable, and then discover what the point is that we are supposed to get. Someone wanted to make *sure* we didn't miss the point of *this* parable!

No doubt the Pharisee here, a man who takes the sovereignty of God quite seriously, is a representative figure. His prayer, "God, I thank you that I am *not* like other people: thieves, rogues, adulterers, or even like this tax collector. . . ." is a blatant statement of what many, if not most of us, have thought surreptitiously, at one time or another. We wouldn't perhaps be so bold as to come out and say it, but we've made those comparisons. We may not be quite as religious as the Pharisee, in terms of our patterns of giving and self-sacrifice; but we sure have noted the deficiencies of others—including some obvious hypocrites–and concluded that, alongside them, we don't look too bad.

So, where is the Pharisee investing his faith? And where do we, when we have such secret thoughts? We're looking at *ourselves*, aren't we? We're saying something like, "Well, I'm not perfect—(unlike those hypocrites who purport to be perfect)—but I don't measure up too badly—*compared to others*, at least. At such times, we're investing our faith in our *own* character or track record. The Publican or Tax Collector, by contrast, doesn't have much of a record to stand on, or run for office upon. So where does he invest his faith? Well, the only place he can: he throws himself upon the mercy and the character of God. "God, be merciful to me, a sinner!

Now, right here, is where entire segments of the Church, past and present, have departed from the teaching of Jesus, who very clearly says at the conclusion of the parable: "I tell you, this man went down to his home justified, rather than the other; for all who exalt themselves will be humbled, but all who humble themselves will be exalted." Hordes of Christians, past and present, have taught that we will be judged or pronounced acceptable before God—or not—based upon our track record—how many wins, how many losses. No, Jesus says in this parable: your being justified before God is *not* a matter of whether you can be proud of and run on your record; it's a matter of recognizing who *God* is.

Some of you are familiar, I expect, with the writings of the Danish philosopher and Christian existentialist, Søren Kierkegaard. He railed in his writings against what he saw as the complacency of the Church of his day and place, where he said, people were Christians "as a matter of course," and as "a mere tomfoolery," when it didn't mean anything to them. Kierkegaard saw the great disparity between the character of God and the character of human beings. We may have been made in the image of God; but we have fallen very far from that, and we need to acknowledge that—as the Tax Collector does in this parable.

Interestingly enough, although Kierkegaard gave the Christians of his day a very hard time—which might make him seem a companion to those moralists today who are preaching a Gospel of salvation by works—nevertheless at the end of all his writings, in his final book, ***Training in Christianity***, Kierkegaard comes to the point, what he calls the Moral of all his writings, and it is this: (I'm paraphrasing for brevity)

> *Be* honest *before God (like this* Tax Collector*)*
> *and* admit *that you have* no *solid foundation of*
> *your* own *on which you can stand. And once you*
> *have* done, *once you have* admitted *to God how*
> *it* is *with you, and thrown yourself upon God's*
> mercy—*then you will find, perhaps to your*
> astonishment, *that God is wonderfully kind and*

gentle—*not condemning you, but* forgiving *you, and empowering you to* love *as you have* been *loved for all eternity.*

Let's consider now the first reading today, from the Book of Jeremiah, where the prophet acknowledges the sins of his people and acts as an intercessor on their behalf. Since Jeremiah *cannot* plead the essential *goodness* of his people, he bases his prayer on the goodness of *God*, saying:

"You, O Lord, are in the midst of us, and we are called by your name. . . ."

"Do not *spurn us, for your* name's *sake; do not* dishonor *your glorious throne. . . . can the* heavens *give showers? Is it not* you, *O Lord our God?* We set our hope on you. . . ."

Our Epistle for today, from 2nd Timothy, shows St. Paul looking back, near the end of his ministry, and acknowledging that he would not have endured, had it not been for the power and faithfulness of God. He concludes by saying, "To him be the glory forever and ever." Elsewhere in his letters, Paul has acknowledged that, though he has tried to live as a good example, he learned at the time of his conversion that Christianity is not a matter of what we have done for God; it is a matter of what *God* has done for *us*. It is knowing the character of God that has kept Paul going—kept him inspired and challenged, not to prove anything, but to respond in gratitude, and to be as faithful as he could be.

This Epistle says that, though we do not face quite the challenges of Paul in witnessing to our own faith, nevertheless all of us are challenged to be true to what we believe—to *express* that faith in our daily living. And what can keep us going? Not a faith in our own good deeds or character, or a fidelity to Biblical commandments, but rather faith that is invested in the very nature of God, the Father of our Lord Jesus Christ.

Here are a few questions I invite you to consider. First, when you go to apply for a job—aside from your resumé of accomplishments and your letters of recommendation, and perhaps your winning personality—what is that intangible factor that an employer is looking for that may be decisive in getting you hired? Is it not your prospective employer's perception that you know that there is something *bigger* than you and your success? Is it not the capacity he or she senses in you to be a *team* player?

Second, what do you look for in a friend? Is it not a quality of faithfulness and reciprocity, so that you know this friend cares about you? Is it not, in short, despite your friend's failings, and acceptance of your failings, a matter of your friend's *character*?

And third, what kind of God will be there for you, when the chips are down, and you have lost the other things, or people, upon whom you were depending for support? Will it be a God who says, "You haven't done enough yet, to impress me? Come back when you have. Or will it be a God who says, in keeping with the teaching of Jesus, "Come on in! I see you're hurting, you're beat up. You're having a hard time trusting. But I love you, the way you are. And I can make you whole."

Bottom Line: Here's a *news flash* for all those who are still trying to prove that they're good enough for God—PUT YOUR FAITH IN THE CHARACTER OF GOD, NOT IN YOUR RESUMÉ. And here's a mantra to keep repeating to yourself: IT'S NOT ABOUT ME; IT'S ABOUT THE GOD WHO IS WAY BIGGER THAN ME, AND WAY KINDER THAN I'LL EVER BE!!

So we say, for the benefit of other Christians and might-be Christians out there, as we testify to the God whom we have found to be faithful and life-giving for us—in the words of Psalm 84, Verse 4: "Happy are the people whose strength is in you! Whose hearts are set on the pilgrims' way. AMEN.

Sermon Thirty-Four

"Standing on the Peak"

March 6, 2011 (Year A) Last Sunday After Epiphany

There is a parallel, it strikes me, between this Sunday—the Last after Epiphany, and the last before Lent—and the Sunday before Advent, in late November, which we call Christ the King. In each case, we're standing on a high point, before we descend to the valley of a penitential season, in preparation for the celebration to follow—although Advent isn't quite as somber as Lent.

Today we stand with Jesus, and his inner circle of disciples— Peter, James, and John—on the Mount of Transfiguration—that peak experience in which the disciples catch a glimpse of who Jesus really is—not only an exceptional man and inspiring teacher but the Son of God. After this vision, they will go back down the mountain, to continue the slog to Jerusalem, where Jesus has already told them he will be killed. Not much to look forward to, in the short run!

In this mountain-top revelation, Jesus appears with the figures of Moses and Elijah, representing the Law and the Prophets—the whole tradition of Israel which provides a context for understanding the identity and mission of Jesus. Both Moses and Elijah had their own mountain-top experiences: Moses in receiving the Laws and instructions for worship; and Elijah in receiving reassurance and a new commission, at a time when he was discouraged and on the run. When Moses came down from the mountain, as we read further in Exodus, and subsequently when he would come back from speaking with God in the Tent of Meeting, his face would be shining from having been in the Presence of God. So when we have our own mountain-top experiences—the times in our lives when we get a glimpse of our own purpose and destiny, and when we see more clearly how God is present with us—we cannot help but be *impacted* by what we have seen. At the very least, we file these snapshot moments away, as the disciples did, and bring them out later when once again we are questioning our significance and what God has in mind for us.

I think we also have Transfiguration experiences in relation to other *people*. One spouse in a couple who have been married for many years, looks at the partner—so familiar, and now suddenly so new—and sees a depth unnoticed before, and God's hand involved in it, and says to himself or herself, "God really did intend you for me. God put you into my life to teach me—humility, for starters—but more than that, what love really means." Sometimes we get these insights belatedly, which is sad—but better late than never. We can have these instances of looking into another human soul with a friend also—or a child, or a parent.

Now, why do you suppose that the Church, in its corporate wisdom, put these readings in the Lectionary for today—the Sunday right before Lent? And why did Jesus take that little group of disciples up the mountain, before they were going to face the music in Jerusalem? It seems pretty clear to me that we have such moments of turning aside from the ordinary, in order to provide clarification and fortification for the challenges ahead. We need clarity, and we need encouragement. It's like a preview of coming attractions, when we're going to be *living* the movie. Lent is both a corporate journey and an individual journey. We journey with Jesus to the Cross—there to face the deepest truths about our life together, and also to encounter the Love that can take us through and sustain us.

I'm sure that for many church members, Lent seems like no big deal: we've seen it before, we've done it before—it's only another season. For other church members, perhaps those who have profited from their previous Lenten experiences, or those who right now are facing challenges in their lives, beyond anything the Church provides them, this time-out, right before we launch the season, is an opportunity to ask ourselves questions such as these:

- "What am I missing in my life right now?"

- "What do I need most?"
- "In what ways would I like to make a new beginning?"

So here is my suggestion this morning. Don't wait until next Sunday, or even Ash Wednesday,—(three days from now)—to ask these questions, and to decide on a Lenten discipline which might be a way of addressing them. If you do wait, it's more likely that whatever discipline you take on will be an after-thought, and a practice undertaken out of a sense of obligation, or because it's traditional, instead of a fresh commitment you're making in conviction that you want to make a new start.

Start thinking today what your Lent this year is going to be about.

- Maybe you want to learn something.
- Maybe you want to form a new habit.
- Maybe you want to let *go* of something that has been *binding* you, and holding you back.

Whatever it is, make it something you can get excited about— something that gives you new energy.

The Church has been around for a long time, and there is much wisdom in its pattern—its annual cycle of observance and teaching. But we can get stale, if we stop bringing our real-life struggles and concerns to God, and tell ourselves: "Oh, it's hopeless; I'll never change." or "I tried that before and it didn't work."

We need to take a few moments to turn aside so that we give God the opportunity to give us a Transfiguration moment: a moment in which we can first say, "Here's how it really *is* with me, God. Here's where I'm *resisting*. Here's what I'm really *afraid* of." And then a moment when we can be still and listen, as Elijah listened, and those disciples did, for that voice from God that can suggest a better way to proceed and a new way of looking at things, and people. There are so many voices competing for our attention today: advertisers, politicians, representatives of good causes, sports announcers, and on and on. But what is the *one* voice to which we need to be *most* attentive?

For Peter, James, and John, who were caught up in a cloud, after being dazzled by seeing Jesus with a brightness and clarity they had never imagined, it was a voice coming out of the cloud, saying to them: "This is my Son . . . listen to him!" Jesus was the authoritative voice on which they were urged henceforth to focus: the voice not only of a man, but the voice of God *among* them. God can speak to *all* of us, in the quietness of our hearts and minds, when we shut off the other voices for a time, and say: "Lord, here is what I need most. Now, what do you want me to do?"

Sermon Thirty-Five

"What Makes Life Worthwhile"

March 27, 2011 (Year A) Lent III

What is it that makes life worthwhile? Health and vigor? Friends? Balance? A winning team? The sense of doing something important?

We could give a number of answers, and all might have some validity in contributing to the good life; but today we're going to look first for an answer in what Jesus said to the woman of Samaria (John 4:5–42), in what is a conversation remarkable for its length, among other things.

Jesus had a number of barriers to overcome in their one-on-one engagement: He was male, she was female; He was a Jew, she was a Samaritan; He was speaking of deep things concerning the Spirit, while her way of thinking was more literal and more concerned with the immediately practical.

We listen in on their conversation through the Gospel today, so Jesus is speaking to us, as well, especially when he speaks of the "Living Water." In his cryptic, mystical comments to the Samaritan woman at the well, I believe that Jesus is extending to all of us, an invitation to come to Him and follow Him, as well as a promise if we do.

This becomes more clear, I think, in the conversation Jesus has with His disciples, after the woman has left to go tell about her encounter. The disciples are urging Jesus to eat something, and his reply to them is as puzzling as some of his comments to the woman. He says, "I have food to eat that you do not know about."

Their first response is very literal. "Did someone bring him food?" So He elaborates: "My food is to do the will of him who sent me. . . ." Then he talks about the harvest—by which he means the opportunities for winning adherents to the kingdom of God, even there, in Samaria.

I'm going to focus on how ministry is at the heart of what Jesus is saying; and I'm going to focus on the ministry of women, in particular.

I found it striking—didn't you?—that two of the three candidates for our new Bishop of Nebraska are women: women of experience and skill and mature faith. The male candidate is a pretty sharp guy also. I have some personal knowledge of all three candidates, and each has strengths that would serve us well. But I'd like to speak for a few moments about the candidate that most people in Nebraska know the least about.

I can't tell you who is the right choice to be our next Bishop. That will be up to the corporate discernment of those who will vote in Hastings on June 4th. What do we need most at this time in our diocesan life, and who is best suited to lead us? These vital questions are a matter for the Spirit and the Body of Christ in Nebraska to decide. But I will tell you something about Margaret Duncan Holt Sammons.

In early 1975 I left Nebraska to accept a call as a curate in a large downtown parish in Kalamazoo, Michigan. The rector was a Scotsman named James Craigie Holt. A retired senior priest in this diocese, Fr. Fred Muller, called me up when he heard I was going there. He congratulated me and said flatly: "Jim Holt is the finest presbyter (priest) in the American Church."

The Holt family was an interesting one. Jim and Joan Holt had five children. The middle three all became medical doctors. The oldest, Margaret, whom we called Peggy, was away when I arrived, serving in the Peace Corps in Africa. I met her upon her return, which as I recall was the next year, 1976. That was also the year when The General Convention of The Episcopal Church, meeting in Minneapolis, did an astounding thing. After years of questioning and foot-dragging, General Convention voted overwhelmingly to approve the ordination of women as priests and bishops.

One of the first postulants for Holy Orders in the Diocese of Western Michigan was Peggy Holt. The bishop of that diocese, a curious amalgam of ancient and modern, had previously opposed the ordination of women—until his two sons, who were both priests, convinced him to change his mind.

For my part—and this is why I'm telling the story—I had already decided that there was no scriptural impediment to ordaining women. Any lingering doubts I had, though, were dissolved when I met Peggy. A more genuine and transparent person I had never met, and I was convinced that her call was of the Holy Spirit. She was the person, more than any other, who clinched the matter for me.

Another woman with a compelling call from God was Hildegard of Bingen, whose story was told in part in a film called VISION, which recently played at the Ross. I hope that a number of you got to see it, or will see it. Hildegard initially did not see herself as strong or a leader, but she could not doubt, and felt compelled to record, the things God was showing her. Her abilities and force of will certainly contributed to her accomplishments; yet fundamentally, Hildegard was a person who simply got into the flow of God's will.

It's a big leap from the life of Hildegard to a fairy tale currently playing at The Grand. It's called BEASTLY—a takeoff on Beauty and the Beast, though the story is different—and even one of my least favorite film critics, Roger Moore, declares it a worthy effort.

In this film, A Big Man on the High School Campus, played by Alex Pettyfer, disses the resident witch, played by Mary-Kate Olsen, who then places on him a disfiguring curse, which can only be removed if he finds, within a year, someone who will freely say to him, "I love you."

To cover his shame, Kyle, the former B.M.O.C., changes his name to Hunter and goes into hiding, where he is ministered to by a blind tutor and a most forgiving housekeeper. The person Hunter hopes will come to love him is Lindy, played by

Vanessa Hudgens. Lindy has her own problems, but is a person of authenticity, with the gift of vision. Remarkably, she had seen something good in Hunter, even when he was Kyle, the jerk. Now she comes to appreciate this new person Kyle is becoming under his disfigurement.

In my own life, I've been blessed from time to time with people who were able to see past my imperfections, and to affirm the person underneath. We all need that kind of ministry; and we need to be engaged in that kind of ministry, as we have opportunity. The ministry of the Church, I believe, is very much a person-to-person ministry, that goes on in workplaces and homes, as well as more visibly in the public eye. It is the members of the household of God—which includes all of you—who show us, by their words and actions, what is real and what is worthwhile. The members of the household of God serve up the "Living Water" for which we all thirst, and which otherwise might elude us. The "Living Water" is manifested in down-to-earth gifts of discernment and kindness, but is powered and guided by a movement much greater—the movement of God's Spirit in the world.

What is that Living Water—that mysterious gift that kept Jesus going? In the simplest terms, it is the flow of God's love—that flow into which we place ourselves when we accept a call to witness to God's Good News, or to minister to human need. And how do we get connected, so that we discover the flow of God's love? We begin in the most human and natural way: we come in our *need*. We are hungry, or thirsty, or scared, or alone, or confused, or all of these. Then we meet someone who can minister to our need; and we find that we in turn have gifts to offer.

We learn to drop our façade of self-sufficiency, as we honestly admit our need, our thirst for the Living Water. Then the creative energy that powers the Universe can move into our lives, to feed us and to equip us, and to move us into sharing our gifts. We find our place in the stream of God's Spirit, so that we can reach out and share the Good News with others, as did the woman of Samaria, and Hildegard of Bingen, and countless others down through the years.

As we get into the flow, the artificial boundaries that separate people—barriers of culture, tradition, looks, and gender roles—drop away and we find community in the Spirit, in God's service.

May God give us all the vision to break down the walls, and to share the Living Water. AMEN.

Sermon Thirty-Six

"Families"

June 10, 2012 (Year B) Proper 5

I'm jumping the gun a little bit here: Father's Day is next Sunday. But as I looked several weeks ago at the Scripture readings for today (Proper 5B, Track One), I saw a thread relating to *FAMILY.* A few words at the outset, then, to put "family" in a contemporary context.

Every family is different from all other families; yet all families try to do some of the same basic things: provide protection and care for their members, and educate their younger members in what they will need to know to get along in the wider society.

The role of parents, whether we are speaking about single parents or two-parent families, is to provide material support, nurture, and advocacy for other family members, and also to set an example in terms of values and character.

It's tougher, we know, for single parents to do all these things, particularly balancing the provision of unconditional love with the provision of boundaries and discipline, when there is no partner to lend a helping hand.

Families are often aided by persons in the larger community—teachers, coaches, other mentors, sometimes grandparents, uncles and aunts. Yet we do place a big load on the shoulders of parents, to provide materially, and to do all these other things. It's a luxury when one parent—father or mother—often these days, it's the father—can stay home a substantial part of the time, to do the hands-on work of parenting and homemaking.

With this contemporary context of family in mind, let's consider some messages which popped up for me as I looked at the readings for today.

In the first reading (1 Sam. 8:14–11, 16–20), the prophet Samuel warns Israel about the pitfalls of getting a king, so that they can be like the other nations. They have so far seen only the advantages.

In families, parents have to stand against the pressures of popular culture, including advertising and peer pressure, which create expectations about what every family should do or have—Whether that is certain kinds of vacations, play equipment, snacks, sports participation—the list goes on and on. Parents are not immune to the temptation to try and keep up with other families.

It's not an easy thing to say to your kids, "Well, you know, we might like to be able to do that, or have that, but we can't afford it right now, and there are other things that we think are more important—such as staying out of debt."

A pressure that comes along with the pressures toward a certain standard of living—which force most families to have two parents working half-time or more outside the home—is time pressure, which tempts many families to reduce their church attendance, or eliminate it entirely, in favor of sports or leisure time.

Parents have to show by their own example that church attendance is important, even if that means giving up some other activity.

Just as Israel had to learn what it didn't yet understand—that being like the other nations comes with a cost—so young family members learn by watching their Christian parents that church participation is not a matter of convenience, but of commitment to building habits of character and values.

A personal note here: both Nan and I had fathers who set a great example in this regard. As a result, speaking for myself, my brother and sister and I all came to believe that the Church is important, and deserving of our time.

Now let's consider that second reading today, from Paul's Second Epistle to the Church at Corinth (4:13–5:1). Paul contrasts that which everyone can see—the outer nature of reality—with the inner reality of faith, where the things most important to us, such as love and ultimate meaning, are realities we can experience but not prove, to anyone's satisfaction other than our own.

Paul declares his own faith, as he says: "we look not at what can be seen, but at what cannot be seen; for what can be seen is temporary, but what cannot be seen is eternal."

It has been well said that "faith has no grandchildren." All that parents can do in instilling the life of faith in their children is to set a good personal example. And I must note that grandparents have, in many cases, taken on the role of parents in setting the example. It remains true that I cannot give you faith through an injection—even as powerful an injection as the Holy Communion—every person has to discover the truth and value of faith in Jesus for himself or herself.

Part of the way we make that discovery is through participation in communities of faith, and through our table fellowship.

The third message I find today for families comes from the Greatest Family of All and has to do with the life of that Family. I'm speaking of the Family of the Holy Trinity: God in Three Persons—Father, Son, and Holy Spirit—working and living as a Unity: Three in One, and One in Three. That's how all families at their best might—working and living as a Unity: Three in One, and One in Three—that's how all families at their best might learn to be.

The way this comes out in the Gospel reading today (Mark 3:20–35) is twofold. First, Jesus warns against insulting His Divine Family by suggesting that the spirit living in Him (by which he has performed miracles and cast out demons) might be an infernal spirit; He refutes that canard by noting that He would have no power to cast out demons, unless that power came from His Heavenly Father.

Then his human family tries to call Him away from His ministry of teaching; and Jesus asks, "Who *are* my mother and my brothers?" He answers his own question by saying: "Here are my mother and my brothers! Whoever does the will of God is my brother and my sister and mother."

Instead of making families smaller, in terms of their outlook and concerns, Jesus makes them bigger. He widens the circle, to include those who are not related by blood or household, but by sharing the vision and calling of a larger enterprise: to bring all people into God's family.

How does this speak to our own situation? It's very tempting to put up walls around our individual families, and to protect ourselves at the expense of others—to say, "our family time is sacred—we don't share it with anyone else!" Churches can do this, as well as individual families. So can nations.

The point is: the concept of family is rooted in the very Being and activity of God; it is not something to be shrunk and worshipped as an idol, independent of everyone else. The purpose of families is not only to care for their own members, but also to teach their members to care for other families, and to help them realize that we are all part of God's Family—the most inclusive and nurturing of all.

It's a demanding thing to be a parent today, and family life has always been challenging; but it is a noble and heavenly calling to nurture and defend families. Only, let's not defend them against *other* families; let's defend them by seeing and living the vision of Jesus—that we are part of God's family—and so are those other folks out there, even the ones who don't know it yet.

Let's make the circle *bigger*, not *smaller*. In the Name of God: Father, Son, and Holy Spirit. Amen.

Sermon Thirty-Seven

"Generosity"

July 1, 2012 (Year B) Proper 8

"As it is written, 'The one who had much did not have too much, and the one who had little did not have too little.'" (2 Cor.8:15)

Imagine that!—St. Paul writing about fairness!

But I want to take it a step further, and talk about generosity, which Paul also mentions. How do you motivate someone to be generous?

There are only two ways I can think of that really work, though other ways have been tried. One is personal example—and Paul cites the example of Jesus. The other is to help the other person get in touch with his reasons to be thankful. Generosity naturally flows from a thankful heart.

Generosity also flows from faith, as contrasted with fear. Our giving—for whatever purpose—reflects our view of God.

Recall the Parable of the Talents (Matt. 25). The master of an estate (whom we understand to be God) goes away and entrusts his property to his servants, to manage in his absence. Not all of the servants receive the same amount to manage, but all have something significant. Two of the servants invest their master's wealth, make a nice return, and are commended upon the master's return.

The third servant is afraid to take a risk, so he buries his share of the property in the ground. When the master returns, the third servant gives this justification for his conduct: "Master, I knew that you were a harsh man. . . ." This was his view of God, and he acted accordingly.

What is our view of God? Notice our first two hymns today. The opening hymn (518) declares that Christ is the cornerstone and sure foundation of the temple we build on earth to honor God, and of the heavenly city which is to come. If Christ is the cornerstone of our faith, what then is our view of God: a despot and avenger? Or a redeemer and reconciler?

Our second hymn (411) declares: "O bless the Lord, my soul! His grace to thee proclaim! . . . O bless the Lord, my soul! His mercies bear in mind! Forget not all his benefits! The Lord to thee is kind. . . ."

Much of our theology is expressed in the words of our hymns, which in turn often come from Hoy Scripture. The words to Hymn 411 are a paraphrase of a portion of Psalm 103.

My point is this: generosity flows from faith, and generosity also reveals character. God's character is shown in God's generosity to us. And God must also to some degree believe in us, to be willing to go so far with us.

It is God's nature to give, and to entrust, as the master in the Parable of the Talents entrusted his property to his servants. What breaks the heart of God, I believe, is to see how little we are able to trust in return, when we are unwilling even to take a risk, and to entrust any of God's wealth to anyone other than ourselves.

Here in America, we like to think of ourselves as a generous country. And it's true that, on occasion, when our hearts are touched by some particular example of need, and not only a threat, Americans do respond. But we don't want to make a policy out of it, lest we should give to the undeserving. We are afraid of losing the wealth that we have come to see as ours, forgetting that we are servants and managers, not the owners.

We have been greatly blessed as a country, with vast natural resources, and a wealth of talented people, who have come here from all corners of the world, to find freedom and opportunity. Jesus says, in Luke 12:48, immediately following a parable not unlike that of the Talents: "From everyone to whom much has been given, much will be demanded."

How does that strike us? Do we see ourselves, as a country and as individuals, accountable to God for the blessings entrusted to us? Does a God who wants and expects a return from us seem petty, and unworthy of our praise? Or may we see such a God as more like a loving parent, who wants us to grow and become more truly Godlike?

We often assume that being Godlike is mostly about exercising power over others. But is it not true to the God that we know through our Lord Jesus Christ, that being Godlike means pouring ourselves out in generosity?

I believe that if America is to realize its potential greatness, we must rediscover the core of our faith, which has to do with joyful receiving and generous giving.

Contrary to what some religious folk believe, America was not explicitly founded as a theocracy, a country under the rule of God. The reason for that is quite simple: our founders were wise enough to know that human rulers are not quite enlightened enough to be trusted with that kind of Godlike power.

Yet it remains true that many of our forebears were people with faith in God—a faith they did not try to cram down the throats of others, but by which they lived lives of faithfulness and generosity.

Jesus boiled the Ten Commandments down into two: Love God with your whole self, and love your neighbor as yourself. If we in our time are to love our many neighbors, at home and abroad, we will need to exert ourselves to know our neighbors quite a bit better than we do at present.

Desmond Tutu, the more-or-less-retired Archbishop of Capetown, South Africa, says that Africans have a word, 'ubuntu' which reflects their understanding that we are not created to live in isolation from our fellow human beings, even when they might be quite different from us.

Ubuntu, says Tutu, literally means, "I am, because we are." In a fuller explanation, he wrote: "Ubuntu is about the essence of being human. It is part of the gift that Africa will give to the world. It embraces hospitality, caring about others, being willing to go the extra mile for the sake of others. We believe that a person is a person through another person, that my humanity is caught up, bound up, in yours. . . ."

Let's return to St. Paul, who wrote: "For you know the generous act of our Lord Jesus Christ, that though he was rich, yet for your sakes he became poor, so that by his poverty you might become rich." (2 Cor: 8:9)

We are invited, and then commissioned, to follow Jesus. When we do follow Him, we find the reward of becoming like Him in His generosity. Generosity blesses the giver, as well as the one who receives. And the one who receives with a thankful heart, is already halfway there.

To be a generous giver is to be like a conduit, open on both ends, so that the life of God may flow through us, and we may become more Christlike, more Godlike.

So may it be, Lord, for us, and for our country.

Sermon Thirty-Eight

"Finding Our Vocation"

September 20, 2015 (Year B) Proper 20

Our Collect for today is an eloquent mini-sermon:

"Grant us, Lord, not to be anxious about earthly things, but to love things heavenly; and even now, while we are placed among things that are passing away, to hold fast to those that shall endure. . . ."

Where are *our* hearts set?

The disciples of Jesus, even while He was preparing them for His death, were arguing about who was the greatest among them.

Where are *our* hearts set?

James, in our Epistle today, offers counsel for the disciples and for us:

> *"Where there is envy and selfish ambition, there will also be disorder. . . .*
>
> *"the wisdom from above is first pure, then peaceable, gentle, willing to yield, full of mercy, and good fruits. . . ."*

Where do we hope to find *our* bliss?

When I was in high school, wondering what my vocation might be, I knew some things I *didn't* want to do; I had no idea yet where my bliss and the world's need would intersect. It is hard for us, I think, to relate our own sense of calling to the vocation of Jesus. He knew He was going to die, and fairly soon; many of us have yet to grapple seriously with that reality. But Jesus wasn't a fatalist, and He didn't see His death as pointless. For Him it was a matter of surrendering to where God was leading Him, so that God might be glorified. The bliss of Jesus was walking in harmony with the will of His Heavenly Father. So in some ways, His path was clear-cut—while most of us find that our own path has not been so clear.

I suppose I could say that my journey to find my vocation began with a *bus ride.* I joined with a busload of other college students from Lincoln—most of them United Methodists; I was the only Episcopalian—to attend the Athens Ecumenical Conference, a worldwide gathering of students, over Christmas of 1963. That's Athens, *Ohio,* not Athens, Greece (or Georgia). I don't recall what specifically led me to make the trip, but by the time I returned, I was pretty sure that it was God doing the leading.

When we arrived at the conference, I walked into an auditorium on the Ohio University campus and heard 3,000 voices singing "Lo, how a rose e'er blooming." It was like a foretaste of heaven. My room-mates for the conference were an Asian student—Chinese, I think—and an African student; we slept in a dorm in a three-tiered bunk—A regular United Nations right there! One of them attended with me the Sunday Eucharist at the Episcopal chapel on campus, a large, colonial-style building. Afterward he said, during a time of group sharing he was impressed by my piety—which surprised me; I had no idea I was making a witness simply by my prayers and participation in the liturgy. The thrust of the conference, titled "For the Life of the World," was not piety, but how our faith engages with the brokenness and injustices of the world. We had some heavyweight speakers: peace activist Bishop Daniel Corrigan, prominent campus chaplain Philip Zabriske, and Alexander Schmemann, the Orthodox theologian. The civil rights movement was underway, and we locked arms in that auditorium and swayed from side to side as we sang, "We shall overcome."

But it wasn't only the speakers or the music that impressed me. It was conversations with individuals, and one in particular: Fay Gemmel, Chaplain at Keene State College, Keene, New Hampshire. Although he was a United Methodist, he was quite drawn to our Anglican tradition and way of worship. In fact, he was the first person to articulate and help *me* to value the sacramental way of thinking, and how it affects the way we engage with the world. He was at that time, more of an Episcopalian than *I* was, and I had grown up in The Episcopal Church. When I returned to Lincoln from that trip, I talked to my college chaplain, George Peek, and said that I wanted to explore a call to the priesthood.

That call would be *tested* over the next several years, as my Bishop decided that I would benefit from *military* experience. I enrolled belatedly in advanced R.O.T.C., got my commission as a Second Lieutenant in the U.S. Army Signal Corps, went to my Army schools, and then—to the horror of my Bishop—was shipped off to Vietnam, as were pretty much all the other young lieutenants at that time (1967). That proved to be a good test of my vocation, because I found myself in some situations where I *had* to rely on God; there wasn't anyone else to help me. I completed my Army tour at the Pentagon, then entered seminary right up the road from there. After seminary, my first assignment was *another* time of testing. But that's a story for another occasion. My point in sharing a bit about my own path to my vocation is that God is often leading us, even when we don't yet understand where or how. How does "the wisdom from above," as James refers to it (3:17), guide our pathway in this world? God doesn't lead us by force, but by *attraction*. God *pulls* us in the direction we need to go. When we are seeking guidance, God provides it—sometimes through a personal encounter with a person we didn't know before, and whom we will never see again. When we are in need, God provides guidance, and by hindsight we can also discern God's protection and merciful provision, when we were out of our depth.

God helps us to engage with the challenges of this world by giving us perspective, and setting our hearts not on "things that are passing away," but on "those that shall endure." However we wind up making our *living*, our *vocation*—our *calling* from God—is not as different from that of Jesus as we might imagine. We are called to set our hearts on following Jesus in all our pursuits, entrusting ourselves to Him, as He entrusted Himself to the Father. So shall we be led to peace, and works of mercy, and the good works to which He has called us.

Sermon Thirty-Nine

"Grace and Call"

February 5, 2017 (Year A) Epiphany. V

As often happens, the Scripture readings this morning are mutually reinforcing, and the effect is cumulative. Let's start with the reading from Isaiah 58 (often read on Ash Wednesday). The theme is: "How do we please God?" God, it seems, speaking through the prophet, has a complaint.

> " . . . *day after day they seek me and delight to know my ways, as* if *they were a nation that practiced* righteousness. . . ."

Meanwhile, it seems the *people* are complaining. The complaint of the people is, "Why do we fast, but you do not see? Why humble ourselves, but you do not notice?" God has a reply for them:

> *"Look, you serve your* own *interest on your fast day, and oppress all your* workers. *Look, you* fast *only to* quarrel *and to* fight. . . . *Such fasting as you do* today *will not make your voice to be heard on high."*

God notes the ritual observances being practiced, and makes light of them. Then God sets forth what would *truly* be pleasing to the Almighty:

> *"Is not* this *the fast that I choose: to loose the bonds of* injustice, *to undo the thongs of the* yoke, *to let the oppressed go* free, *and to* break *every yoke? Is it not to share your bread with the* hungry, *and bring the homeless* poor *into your house. . . .* Then *your light will break forth like the dawn. . . . Then you shall* call, *and the Lord will* answer. . . ."

It seems that the righteousness God is seeking from us is more than the faithful observance of religious practices that ignore one's neighbor. "Righteousness," which means right *relationship* with

God, involves our other relationships as *well. True* religion, whether Judaism or Christianity, or—(dare we say it?)—some *other* religion, is not a matter of saving *ourselves.* Our call is *greater* than that.

What *is* our call? We'll get to that presently. We misread the Collect for today, if we think it's an expression of the "prosperity Gospel"—that is, the notion that our material blessings are a sign of God's favor. Our Collect for today, asks God to set us free from the bonds of our sins, and to give us the liberty of abundant life—but not *any* abundant life, rather "that abundant life with (God) has made known to us in our Savior Jesus Christ. . . ."

Our Psalm today speaks not only of God's blessings to those "who fear the Lord and . . . delight in his commandments," but also of their virtues of generosity and justice, including giving "freely to the poor. . . ."

Now, we may ask, how do we know what God requires, and what God has planned for us? Let's move to the Epistle, from 1 Cor. 2. Paul says, "When I came to you, brothers and sisters, I did not come proclaiming the mystery of God to you in lofty words or wisdom. For I decided to know nothing among you except Jesus Christ, and him crucified. I came to you in weakness and in fear and in much trembling. My speech and my proclamation were not with plausible words of wisdom, but with a demonstration of the Spirit and of power. . . ." He goes on to say: "We speak God's wisdom . . . revealed to us through the Spirit. . . ."

How do we know God's will, and God's plans for us? Two answers: Jesus, and the Spirit. So now we come to the question: "What is our call?" And here we turn to today's Gospel, from the 5th chapter of St. Matthew: we are to be salt and light to the world. That is, we are to live in a way that shows forth the glory of God—God's *flavor* and God's *illumination.*

And then we come to the kicker—Matthew 5:20. Jesus says: "I tell you, unless your righteousness *exceeds* that of the scribes and Pharisees (that is, those people who were scrupulously laboring to know and to meet God's requirements), you will *never* enter the kingdom of heaven." At that point, it would be easy to feel sucker-punched, and to sputter, "But that's *impossible!*" And that's the *point*. We don't enter the kingdom of heaven, the condition of being totally blessed and totally in tune with God, by our own efforts. We don't save ourselves, and we don't enter as *individuals*. We enter in company with *all* the saints, or we don't enter at all.

We don't enter because we are good people, who have met every requirement. We enter because we have put our trust in a great God—the hidden God revealed by Jesus and the Spirit, and in the grace—that is, the free and unmerited favor which has been conveyed to us, as we dwell within the goodness of God, Father, Son, and Holy Spirit, with all the rest of God's people.

A movie currently playing locally is ***The Founder***, starring Michael Keaton as Ray Kroc, builder of the McDonald's fast food empire. I suspect we've all eaten at McDonald's, not once but many times. It certainly has been a boon to travelers, especially families with children. But Ray Kroc didn't do it all by himself: he had key helpers along the way, from the prototype business he copied, to innovators who showed him how to be more efficient. Sad to say, not all of them got the rewards that were rightfully theirs.

Our call from God is not to be a *winner*, that is, to get across the finish line of life ahead of *others*; and it is not to save *ourselves*. We are called to be salt and light in a world where those gifts are very much needed, and by sharing them, as best we can, to show forth the great goodness of God—the love and the power of God.

Sermon Forty

"Christmas People"

December 18, 2016 (Year A) Advent IV

Our Collect for today helps us to zero in on the central *purpose* of the feast we are preparing to celebrate: the Feast of the Incarnation—God's taking human flesh and coming to live among us. The Collect, which repeats the Advent note of preparation in *these* words also states the *purpose* of God's action" "that (Jesus) may find in us a mansion prepared for *himself.* . . ."

God is coming to *live in us.* That is an *awesome* prospect! God's greatest miracle—coming to live in a human life—is to be ongoing. God is not coming simply to visit, but to make a home in us. When we contemplate such a staggering intention, it makes the various preparations we make for other human visitors, even important ones, seem trivial by comparison. Cooking, cleaning, decluttering: these are all worthwhile preparations. But they **pale** before the preparation of our *hearts* to receive the King of Kings and the Lord of Lords.

The prophet Isaiah spoke of a sign to be given by God: a young woman shall bear a son, and he will be called Immanuel, which means "God (is) with us." An angel appeared to Joseph in a dream and said that Mary would bear a son, and he will be named Jesus, which means "God *saves.*" If we are looking for a sign of what God is doing in our world today, the sign has already been given. It is not a new leader, but one who already is in us and among us, by virtue of the Incarnation and our baptism. We are already the recipients of grace, which is God's favor and help, unmerited and often unrecognized. Will we recognize the presence of Jesus, and fully open ourselves to Him in this season and in the days to come?

In mid-October of this year, I saw a film at the Ross which was generally unheralded, and mostly unnoticed. Its title was *The*

Vessel. Martin Sheen co-starred as Fr. Douglas, a priest in a small seaside town. He was in a tough position. The people in that town felt that they were under a curse, because years before, a huge tidal wave had struck one morning when all the children were in school, and had swept them all away. The people in the town felt that they had no *future*. Their dreams and hopes had been taken away. They wore black, and no one wanted to have children. They were looking for some sign that God hadn't abandoned them. They looked first to the priest, but although he was a good shepherd, he had no special magic for them.

Then they looked to Leo, a young man who was a sort of living miracle, since he had survived an apparent drowning that should have killed him. Responding to their pleas, Leo builds a makeshift boat, tries to sail in it, and when it fails, he starts swimming hopelessly out to sea. His mother, who has been in a wordless reverie since her other son died in the tidal wave, suddenly springs into action. She calls out Leo's name, and starts swimming out to him. That wakes up the town. Leo and his girlfriend prepare to leave town, to find a new life, and another couple decides to conceive a child.

The Vessel doesn't spell out the message; it leaves that up to the viewers. But it is a kind of parable about how new life can emerge, even after hope has been lost. What Leo and Fr. Douglas both contribute, even though neither is successful in providing a sign, is that they offer themselves—just as we do every Sunday in the Eucharist. In so doing, they open themselves to the possibility that *God* may do something, in response to their offering.

In our Epistle today, we see the difference between being a *disciple* of Jesus—that is, one who tries to follow his teaching and example—and being an *apostle*, which means accepting the commission of being *sent out*, as Paul was sent out to share his message. Our call is really to do both: to be faithful followers and to be proclaimers.

The four candles in the Advent wreath, as we have been reminded in this season, are signs of the new life which we anticipate in the coming of Jesus. They stand for Hope, Peace, Joy, and Love. These are also the marks of a Christian—one who lives in Hope and brings Hope; one who lives in Peace and helps to bring Peace; one who lives in Joy and brings Joy; one who lives in Love and brings Love. These are not simply *ideals* to which we aspire; they are signs that Jesus has made a home in us, and that we now are moved to share that Good News with others—to be apostles of the Good News, and not only disciples.

We are sent, by virtue of the Incarnation and our baptism into the Body of Christ, to be lights in a world where there is often darkness. Our calling is not less than to be *Christmas people*, bringing Hope, Peace, Joy, and Love into other lives, because those gifts have made a home in us. We do not have any *magic*; all we have to give is ourselves, as God gave His very self to a needy world.

As Mary and Joseph in obedience offered themselves to help bring new life into the world, the life that was to become a sign and a beacon to the world, so each of us today, as we prepare and open ourselves to the lifegiving Good News of Christmas, may be bearers of the light that assures the world that God saves, and God is with us. Welcome the sign, and be the sign which the world awaits; let Hope, Peace, Joy, and the Love of Jesus live in you. Amen.

ACKNOWLEDGEMENTS

Many thanks to Robbi Ryan, my transcriptionist, designer and publisher, for her cheerful and resourceful assistance. Without her help, this collection would not have come into being.

Thanks to all who have been my listeners and encouragers over the years, including my wife Nan, as I have grown in my personal appropriation and boldness in preaching the Living Word.

—Donald G. Hanway